New
CHOCOLATE
CLASSICS

New CHOCOLATE CLASSICS

Over 100 of Your Favorite Recipes
Now Irresistibly in
Chocolate

Diana Dalsass

W. W. NORTON & COMPANY
New York • London

For information about permission to reproduce selections from this book, write to Permissions, W. W. Norton & Company, Inc., 500 Fifth Avenue, New York, NY 10110.

The text of this book is composed in Souvenir
with the display set in Goudy Sans and Windsor
Composition by Charlotte Staub
Manufacturing by the Courier Companies
Botanical drawings and book design by Charlotte Staub

Library of Congress Cataloging-in-Publication Data

Dalsass, Diana.
        New chocolate classics : over 100 of your favorite recipes now
    irresistibly in chocolate / Diana Dalsass.
            p.   cm.
        Includes index.
        ISBN 0-393-31881-8 (pbk.)
        1. Cookery (Chocolate) 2. Desserts.   I. Title.
        TX767.C5D35   1999
    641.6'374—dc21   98-31268
                                                      CIP

W. W. Norton & Company, Inc., 500 Fifth Avenue, New York, N.Y. 10110
http://www.wwnorton.com

W. W. Norton & Company Ltd., 10 Coptic Street, London WC1A 1PU

1 2 3 4 5 6 7 8 9 0

CONTENTS

THE COOKIE CRUMBLES TO CHOCOLATE 97

WOW! IS THAT CHOCOLATE IN MY BREAD? 121

UNIQUELY CHOCOLATE CREATIONS 141

INDEX 153

INTRODUCTION

I am more passionate about chocolate than anyone else I know. Much of my life has been devoted to finding new chocolate sensations, and I never pass up an opportunity to taste unique chocolate combinations, no matter how odd they may sound. For example, at a wonderful Manhattan restaurant, Aureole, I ordered a chocolate-tarragon dessert. I remember nothing else about the meal, but the taste of that brownie filled with warm fudge sauce infused with the haunting aroma of tarragon will linger forever in my mind.

As a result of this lifelong quest, I began to imagine the flavors of favorite non-chocolate desserts when transformed into chocolate versions of themselves. In my mind, I could "taste" Chocolate Coconut Cream Pie, Chocolate Tiramisu, and Chocolate Cannoli. As my fantasies played out, I realized that innumerable classic desserts would be even more delectable with the addition of chocolate.

This book is the felicitous result of that pursuit: Dozens of favorite desserts in a new chocolate incarnation.

The book contains recipes, adapted to chocolate, for traditional desserts from many countries, such as Greek Baklava, Italian Zabaglione, British Scones, and French Madelines.

Also included in the book are many American favorites, again transformed to chocolate, such as Tapioca Pudding, Boston Cream Pie, Gingerbread, and Apple Brown Betty.

Finally, there are wonderful recipes from the 1950s, which are even better now in their chocolate versions, such as Icebox Cake, Baked Alaska, and Ambrosia.

All of these recipes have been altered to make them as chocolaty as possible. This meant my having to adjust most of the other ingredients, including the quantities of butter, sugar, flour, and liquid. Often, several attempts were needed before I developed the best chocolate version of a recipe.

What you will find in this book was worth all the effort—an entirely new collection of desserts that are delectably chocolate.

Chocolate as an Ingredient

Chocolate for making desserts comes in one of three primary forms: unsweetened chocolate, semi-sweet chocolate, and unsweetened cocoa powder.

UNSWEETENED CHOCOLATE

Unsweetened chocolate, which is most commonly made by Baker's, is individually wrapped in 1-ounce squares, with 8 squares to a box.

Recipes for unsweetened chocolate usually call for the chocolate to be melted. This can be done in a microwave oven or in a small saucepan on top of the stove. If using the stovetop method, the chocolate must be melted over a very low heat to prevent it from burning. Some people prefer to use a double boiler, which makes it almost impossible for the chocolate to burn. But I find this to be a nuisance, unless I need the double boiler for a later step in the recipe.

If a recipe calls for unsweetened chocolate and you have none on hand (or not enough), you may substitute unsweetened cocoa powder for the chocolate. The substitution is:

For each square of unsweetened chocolate, use 3 tablespoons unsweetened cocoa powder plus 1 tablespoon butter or margarine.

To add the chocolate substitution to the recipe, you may melt the butter and then stir in the cocoa. Alternatively, you may add the extra butter along with the rest of the butter called for in the recipe, and mix the cocoa with the dry ingredients. I prefer this latter method, as it saves on having to wash an extra sauce-pan.

The reason this substitution works is because the two main components of unsweetened chocolate are cocoa and cocoa butter.

Cocoa butter is quite expensive, so baking with the squares of unsweetened chocolate is somewhat more costly than substituting cocoa plus ordinary butter or margarine. Thus, I often use the substitution for chocolate, even when I haven't run out of this ingredient.

To test whether substituting cocoa for chocolate actually *does* make a detectable difference in the final result, I made two batches of brownies that were identical, except that one was prepared with chocolate and the other with cocoa plus extra butter.

Family members and friends were given one of each brownie and asked to taste them, with no other explanation given. They were then asked whether they found any difference between the two brownies and, if so, which they preferred.

Everyone was able to taste a difference between the two batches of brownies. The majority of tasters preferred the brownies made with the chocolate, saying it gave a more candylike flavor. However, the cocoa brownies were favored by some, who felt that these were more intensely chocolate.

Bottom line: Your dessert will come out a little different if you substitute cocoa for chocolate. But the dessert will probably taste almost as delicious and, depending on your own tastes, may be even more appealing. So if you have no chocolate on hand or wish to economize, feel comfortable substituting cocoa.

SEMI-SWEET CHOCOLATE

The best known form of this ingredient is chocolate chips or, more formally, semi-sweet chocolate morsels. As anyone knows who has ever tried to resist eating these right out of the bag, semi-sweet chocolate tastes and, in fact, is just like candy. That's why this chocolate adds such a deliciously sweet flavor to cookies, cakes, ice cream, and a myriad of other desserts.

But as is the case with all chocolate candy, the quality of semi-sweet chocolate can vary greatly. Most of the recipes in this book that call for semi-sweet chocolate specify chocolate morsels. This is because all home bakers buy them regularly. If you do use chocolate morsels, buy from a company whose name you know, as some of the store-name brands taste overly waxy.

When I make chocolate desserts, I generally use a higher quality semi-sweet chocolate. Such chocolate is found in specialty food stores, usually in bars (such as those made by Lindt or Tobler). (The bars can be chopped by hand or in a food processor until they are the approximate size of the usual chocolate chips.) Such bars are more expensive than using ordinary chocolate chips purchased at the supermarket. Whether you wish to spend the additional money depends on how much you, personally, are able to detect the difference in the quality of the chocolates.

All true chocoholics should know about Hawaiian Vintage chocolate, which is used by many top restaurants in their chocolate desserts. Although this chocolate is very expensive and requires a minimum purchase of 8 pounds (which comes in the form of pastilles, which are like very large chocolate chips), I have come to love its flavor and texture, and so prefer it to all other brands of semi-sweet chocolate. Hawaiian Vintage chocolate is available by mail order from Continental Foods (800-345-1543).

UNSWEETENED COCOA POWDER

Cocoa, of course, is what gives chocolate its distinctive flavor. Alone, cocoa is not appealing, as it is bitter, dry, and powdery. But when combined with other ingredients, cocoa produces intensely chocolate cakes, cookies, brownies, candies, and so on.

Although there are hundreds of cocoas available to food professionals, only two types are generally found in grocery stores—alkalized (or Dutch-process) and non-alkalized, which refer to the method of processing the cocoa beans. Hershey's Cocoa is non-alkalized, while Droste's is the best-known brand of alkalized cocoa. Recipes designed to appeal to "gourmets" often specify using alkalized cocoa.

Since alkalized cocoa is harder to locate and more expensive, I decided to conduct a taste comparison of the two. I made identical batches of brownies. In one batch, I used Hershey's Cocoa; the other batch contained the Williams-Sonoma brand of alkalized cocoa.

It was difficult for the taste test to be "blind," as the brownies looked distinctly different, with the ones containing the alkalized cocoa appearing much darker in color.

Since I usually associate a dark color with an increased chocolate flavor, I fully expected these brownies to be more intensely chocolaty. However, just the opposite was true. The brownies made with Hershey's Cocoa tasted exactly like wonderful brownies should — they were rich, dark, chewy, and chocolaty.

The brownies made with the alkalized cocoa were more moist and less chewy, and the chocolate flavor was less pronounced. The bars were delicious, but they just didn't taste quite like brownies.

Bottom line: You may wish to experiment to see which type of cocoa you prefer. For someone who wants the traditional, intense chocolate flavor, I recommend using Hershey's. For a chocolate flavor that's more subtle, perhaps even intriguing, use the alkalized cocoa. Either way, every recipe in this book calling for cocoa will come out great!

PIES
for
CHOCOHOLICS

Coconut Cream Pie

*C*oconut Cream Pie is one of my husband's favorite desserts, and he orders it in restaurants whenever it's available. But even he has to admit that the conversion to Chocolate Coconut Cream Pie is even better. The filling is light, yet rich—similar to a dark chocolate mousse—with toasted coconut scattered throughout and on top. As a final improvement, chocolate cookies are used for the crumb crust.

This filling is so delicate that it needs several hours of chilling in order to firm up sufficiently to cut the pie. Therefore, plan to make the pie early on the day you intend to serve it or a day in advance.

CHOCOLATE CRUMB CRUST
1½ cups finely crushed chocolate cookie crumbs (a 9-ounce box of Nabisco's Famous Chocolate Wafers)
6 tablespoons butter, melted

FILLING
1⅓ cups shredded coconut
3½ cups whole milk, divided
1 envelope unflavored gelatin
1½ cups sugar
¼ cup cornstarch
4 egg yolks
4 1-ounce squares unsweetened chocolate
2 teaspoons vanilla
1 cup heavy or whipping cream

Yield: 12 servings

1. Prepare the crumb crust: Preheat the oven to 300°F. In a bowl, stir together the cookie crumbs and melted butter. Press evenly into the bottom and up the sides of a deep dish 9-inch pie plate. Bake for 15 minutes. Transfer the pan to a rack to cool. Do not turn off the oven.

2. Spread the coconut on an ungreased cookie sheet. Bake about 8 minutes, stirring once, or until the coconut is lightly toasted. Transfer the coconut to a dinner plate and let cool. (Turn off the oven.)

3. In a large mixing bowl, stir together ⅓ cup milk and the gelatin. Let sit for 5 minutes. Add the sugar, cornstarch, and egg yolks and mix well.

4. Pour the remaining milk into a saucepan. Add the chocolate. Cook over a medium heat, stirring occasionally, until the chocolate has melted. Continue cooking until the milk is scalded (little bubbles will appear at the edge of the saucepan, but the milk will not come to a full boil).

5. Remove the saucepan from the heat. Beat about a half cup of the chocolate milk mixture into the bowl with the egg yolks. Now add the chocolate milk/egg yolk mixture to the contents of the saucepan. Cook, stirring constantly,

over a low heat until the mixture becomes thickened. This will take about 15 minutes. Stir in the vanilla.

6. Transfer the contents of the saucepan to a clean bowl. Cover with plastic wrap placed directly on the filling. (This prevents a "skin" from forming.) Chill the mixture until cold.

7. When the cooked mixture is nearly chilled, beat the heavy cream until whipped. Fold into the chilled mixture. Stir in about half the coconut.

8. Pour the filling into the crust. Sprinkle with the remaining coconut. Chill several hours before serving.

Eggnog Pie

*T*his is an old-fashioned recipe that definitely deserves a revival. The flavors of eggnog—milk or cream, egg yolks, rum, and nutmeg—are combined in a mousse-like pie filling to make a very appealing dessert. This version begins with a chocolate crust and flavors the filling with chocolate, which adds to its richness.

CHOCOLATE PASTRY CRUST
1½ cups flour
½ cup sugar
¼ cup unsweetened cocoa powder, sifted if lumpy
pinch of salt
6 tablespoons butter or margarine
3 to 4 tablespoons ice water

FILLING
1 cup milk
3 eggs
¾ cup sugar
pinch of salt
⅛ teaspoon nutmeg
⅓ cup unsweetened cocoa powder
1 envelope unflavored gelatin
2 tablespoons water
2 tablespoons dark rum
1 teaspoon vanilla
1 cup heavy or whipping cream

Yield: 8 to 10 servings

1. Prepare the crust: In a large bowl, stir together the flour, sugar, cocoa, and salt. With a pastry cutter, 2 knives, or your fingertips, cut in the butter or margarine until the texture is that of coarse meal. Add just enough water for the ingredients to hold together. Form the dough into a ball and refrigerate for 1 hour.
2. Preheat the oven to 325°F.
3. On a lightly floured surface, roll out the dough to fit the bottom and sides of a 9-inch deep dish pie plate. Fit the dough into the pie plate, and prick it in several places on the bottom and sides with a fork.
4. Bake the pie crust for 25 minutes, or until the dough is cooked and lightly browned. Transfer the pie plate to a rack to cool. Let cool completely before filling the pie.
5. In the meantime, prepare the filling: Place the milk in the top of a double boiler. Heat directly on the burner to scalding (just before it begins to boil). Then transfer over boiling water in the double boiler.
6. In a bowl, using a wire whisk, beat together the eggs, sugar, salt, nutmeg, and cocoa. Add to the scalded milk. Cook, stirring constantly, until a light custard forms. (The mixture will be thick enough to coat a spoon.)
7. Mix together the gelatin and water. Let stand for 5 minutes to soften the gelatin. Add to the custard mixture. Stir in the rum and vanilla.

8. Transfer the custard mixture to a bowl, and place plastic wrap directly on the mixture to prevent a "skin" from forming. Chill until cold.
9. In a bowl, beat the heavy cream until whipped. Fold the whipped cream into the custard mixture. Pour into the pie crust. Chill the pie until set for at least 2 hours.

Key Lime Pie

*D*eveloping this pie recipe required lots of experimentation. Again and again, I tried different proportions for the filling, but each time, it was too runny. The reason I persisted was that the flavor of the pie was incomparably delicious—dark, rich, and chocolaty, with the sharp, tangy contrast of fresh lime. After about five attempts, this recipe was developed, which means that you can enjoy it on your very first try.

CHOCOLATE PASTRY CRUST
1 recipe Chocolate Pastry Crust from Eggnog Pie (page 16)
1 teaspoon finely grated lime rind

FILLING
1½ cups sugar
⅓ cup cornstarch
½ cup unsweetened cocoa powder
3 egg yolks
½ cup milk
1 tablespoon butter or margarine
⅓ cup freshly squeezed lime juice
1 8-ounce container sour cream

Yield: 10 to 12 servings

1. Prepare and bake the pie crust according to the recipe for Eggnog Pie. (Add the lime rind along with the dry ingredients.)
2. In a heavy saucepan, stir together the sugar, cornstarch, and cocoa. In a small bowl, beat together the egg yolks and milk. Add to the cocoa mixture and stir well. Add the butter. Cook, stirring frequently, over a medium heat until the mixture comes to a boil. Add the lime juice and boil, stirring constantly, for 2 minutes.
3. Transfer the contents of the saucepan to a bowl and stir in the sour cream. Let sit until the mixture nearly comes to room temperature.
4. Pour the filling into the pie crust. Cover the pie and chill for several hours before serving.

Pumpkin Pie

*F*or anyone who ever found ordinary pumpkin pie a boring Thanksgiving offering, this version provides a completely new taste sensation. The chocolate almost, but not completely, disguises the pumpkin flavor, while the pumpkin lends a buttery, smooth texture. The combination—baked in a cookie-like chocolate crust—is totally delightful.

CHOCOLATE PASTRY CRUST
- **1 recipe Chocolate Pastry Crust from Eggnog Pie (page 16)**

FILLING
- **1 1-pound can solid pack pumpkin (not pumpkin pie filling)**
- **2 eggs beaten**
- **1 cup sugar**
- **3 1-ounce squares unsweetened chocolate, melted**
- **½ teaspoon cinnamon**
- **¼ teaspoon ginger**
- **¼ teaspoon ground cloves**
- **¼ teaspoon salt**
- **1 12-ounce can evaporated milk**

Yield: 8 servings

1. Prepare the pie crust according to the recipe for Eggnog Pie, but do not bake it.
2. Preheat the oven to 425°F.
3. In a large bowl, mix together all the ingredients for the pie filling. Pour into the crust.
4. Place the pie in the oven and bake for 15 minutes. Lower the oven temperature to 350°F. Bake the pie for 1¼ hours longer, or until a knife inserted in the center comes out clean.
5. Let the pie cool on a rack to room temperature and chill well before serving.

Vinegar Pie

*V*inegar Pie is an early American recipe, dating back to when fresh fruit was difficult to obtain. Craving the flavor of apples, housewives made a highly economical pie with apple cider vinegar. Looking at the ingredients—1/2 cup vinegar and 2 cups water, among others—it's hard to imagine that this pie could taste good. But, in fact, it is absolutely delicious—thick and custardy, like the filling of a pecan pie. And, of course, Chocolate Vinegar Pie is even richer and more flavorful.

CHOCOLATE PASTRY CRUST
1 recipe Chocolate Pastry Crust from Eggnog Pie (page 16)

FILLING
1¾ cups sugar
¼ cup flour
½ cup cider vinegar
2 cups water
2 1-ounce squares unsweetened chocolate
3 eggs
1 tablespoon butter

Yield: 10 to 12 servings

1. Prepare the pie crust according to the recipe for Eggnog Pie, but bake the crust for 8 minutes at 400°F.
2. Place the sugar and flour in a heavy saucepan and stir together well. Stir in the vinegar. Add the water and chocolate. Cook over a medium heat, stirring occasionally, until the chocolate has melted and the mixture comes to a boil. Let boil for 1 minute, stirring constantly. Remove from the heat.
3. Preheat the oven to 475°F.
4. In a small bowl, beat the eggs well. Gradually beat in about 1 cup of the hot liquid, stirring constantly. Add the egg mixture to the saucepan, and then add the butter. Stir until melted.
5. Pour the filling into the pie crust. Bake for 10 minutes. Lower the heat to 350°F and bake for 35 minutes longer. The filling will be somewhat liquidy but will firm up as it cools. Transfer the pie to a rack and let cool completely.

Gravel Pie

*T*his Pennsylvania Dutch dessert layers buttered cookie crumbs over a butterscotch filling for a pie that does, indeed, resemble gravel. When turned to chocolate, the filling looks more like tar than gravel. The pie is incredibly dark, rich, and delicious—a not-to-be-missed dessert for chocoholics!

CHOCOLATE PASTRY CRUST
1 recipe Chocolate Pastry Crust from Eggnog Pie (page 16)

FILLING
1 cup brown sugar, preferably dark
3 eggs
½ cup water
½ cup semi-sweet chocolate morsels
⅓ cup flour
¼ cup unsweetened cocoa powder
¼ cup sugar
½ teaspoon cinnamon
¼ teaspoon nutmeg
⅛ teaspoon ginger
⅓ cup (5⅓ tablespoons) butter, cut into tiny pieces
1 cup crushed chocolate cookies

Yield: 8 to 10 servings

1. Prepare and bake the pie crust according to the recipe for Eggnog Pie.
2. Preheat the oven to 325°F.
3. In the top of a double boiler, beat the brown sugar with the eggs. Stir in the water. Cook over boiling water, stirring frequently, until the mixture is thick and syrupy. Transfer to a bowl and let cool slightly.
4. Sprinkle the chocolate morsels over the bottom of the pie crust. Pour the cooked filling over the morsels.
5. In a small bowl, stir together the flour, cocoa, sugar, cinnamon, nutmeg, and ginger.
6. Sprinkle one-third of the flour mixture over the filling. Cover with one-third of the butter, then one-third of the cookie crumbs. Repeat these layers twice more.
7. Bake the pie for 30 minutes. Transfer to a rack and let cool to room temperature before serving.

Jefferson Davis Pie

*J*efferson Davis Pie is an old southern recipe that deserves to be revived. The pie filling is a fudgy butterscotch mixture that's packed with dates, raisins, and pecans. A thin meringue topping adds a highly attractive finish to the pie. Chocolate Jefferson Davis Pie starts with a chocolate pie crust and finishes with a chocolate meringue. The filling between is the fudgiest chocolate imaginable!

CHOCOLATE PASTRY CRUST
1 recipe Chocolate Pastry Crust from Eggnog Pie (page 16)

FILLING
1 stick butter or margarine, softened
2 cups brown sugar, preferably dark
4 egg yolks
3 1-ounce squares unsweetened chocolate, melted
1 cup heavy or whipping cream
2 tablespoons flour
1 teaspoon cinnamon
½ teaspoon nutmeg
½ cup raisins
½ cup chopped dates
½ cup chopped pecans

MERINGUE
2 egg whites
¼ teaspoon cream of tartar
6 tablespoons sugar
3 tablespoons unsweetened cocoa powder

Yield: 10 to 12 servings

1. Prepare the pie crust according to the recipe for Eggnog Pie, but do not bake it.
2. Preheat the oven to 325°F.
3. In a large bowl, cream the butter and brown sugar, continuing to beat until the sugar is fully incorporated. Beat in the egg yolks, then the chocolate and cream. Beat in the flour, cinnamon, and nutmeg. Stir in the raisins, dates, and pecans.
4. Spread the filling evenly in the pie crust. Bake the pie for about 1 hour, or until the filling is set. A toothpick inserted in the center will come out almost, but not completely, clean.
5. When the pie is nearly finished baking, make the meringue topping. Beat the egg whites with the cream of tartar until stiff. Gradually beat in the sugar, continuing to beat until the mixture is glossy. Beat in the cocoa.
6. Spread the meringue evenly over the baked pie. Return to the oven and bake for 15 minutes longer.
7. Transfer the pie to a rack and cool. Serve at room temperature. Leftover pie should be refrigerated.

Frangipane Tart

*F*rangipane Tart, with its filling of almond paste and fresh fruit, makes a lovely summertime dessert. This recipe starts with a chocolate graham cracker crust and has a chocolate-almond filling, which is enhanced by delicate apricots. The tart looks as delicious as it tastes.

CHOCOLATE PASTRY CRUST
1 inner package chocolate graham crackers, crushed (about 1½ cups)
6 tablespoons butter or margarine, melted

FILLING
1 8-ounce can almond paste
3 tablespoons butter or margarine, softened
¾ cup sugar
2 eggs
2 1-ounce squares unsweetened chocolate, melted
1 teaspoon vanilla
½ cup flour
1 pound fresh apricots (about 8), quartered

Yield: 10 servings

1. Mix together the graham crumbs and butter. Press the mixture into a 9-inch pie plate. Chill the crust for at least 1 hour.
2. Preheat the oven to 350°F.
3. The filling is most easily prepared in a food processor, but if you don't have a food processor, use an electric mixer. Place the almond paste, butter, and sugar in the bowl of the food processor and process until smooth. Add the eggs and process until incorporated. Add the chocolate and process again. Add the vanilla and flour. Process, using quick on-and-off motions, until the flour is incorporated.
4. Spread the filling evenly in the prepared crust. Place the apricots, cut side down, in concentric circles over the filling.
5. Bake the tart for 50 to 60 minutes, or until the filling is set and a toothpick inserted in the center comes out almost, but not completely, clean.
6. Transfer the tart to a rack to cool. This is best served at room temperature.

German Sponge Tart

*T*his is a truly incredible dessert. In its traditional form, the tart is delicious but not exceptionally special: a pastry crust, filled with ground nuts and jam, and covered with a sponge cake. When transformed to chocolate, however, the dessert's character changes entirely. The crust is a rich chocolate pastry (rather like a shortbread cookie). This is filled with black cherry preserves and covered with a mixture of ground nuts and semi-sweet chocolate, all of which is topped by a brownie-like cake.

RICH CHOCOLATE PASTRY CRUST
1½ sticks (¾ cup) butter, softened
½ cup sugar
2 egg yolks
1¾ cups flour
⅓ cup unsweetened cocoa powder,
   sifted if lumpy
¼ teaspoon salt

FILLING
1 cup black cherry preserves
½ cup ground walnuts
½ cup ground semi-sweet chocolate
1 teaspoon cinnamon
4 eggs, separated
¾ cup sugar, divided
1 teaspoon vanilla
3 tablespoons flour
3 tablespoons cornstarch
¼ cup unsweetened cocoa powder,
   sifted if lumpy

Yield: 12 servings

1. Butter a deep dish 9-inch pie plate.
2. Prepare the crust: In a large bowl, cream the butter and sugar, continuing to beat until the sugar is fully incorporated. Beat in the egg yolks. In another bowl, stir together the flour, cocoa, and salt. Add to the butter mixture, beating or stirring only until the dry ingredients are incorporated.
3. Pat the dough into the pie plate, pressing it evenly on the bottom and up the sides. Chill the dough for at least 1 hour.
4. Preheat the oven to 350°F.
5. Spread the cherry preserves over the bottom of the pie.
6. Stir together the ground nuts, chocolate, and cinnamon. Sprinkle over the preserves.
7. In a bowl, beat the egg whites until stiff. Gradually add ¼ cup sugar and continue beating until the mixture is thick and glossy.
8. In another bowl, beat the egg yolks. Gradually beat in the remaining ½ cup sugar, continuing to beat until the mixture is thick and pale. Beat in the vanilla.
9. In a small bowl, stir together the flour, cornstarch, and cocoa. Add to the egg yolk mixture, stirring until the dry ingredients are incorporated. The mixture will be very thick.

10. Add about half the egg whites to the chocolate mixture and stir well. This will lighten the batter so you can now fold in the remaining egg whites gently but thoroughly.

11. Turn the batter into the pie pan. Bake the tart for about 55 minutes, or until a toothpick inserted in the center of the pie comes out clean.

12. Transfer the tart to a rack to cool. Serve at room temperature.

BEYOND
the
PASTRY SHOP

Baklava

*B*aklava is that wonderful Greek pastry, made with unbelievably thin layers of phyllo dough, filled with walnuts and topped with a honey syrup. Chocolate Baklava is even more heavenly, with semi-sweet chocolate replacing a portion of the usual ground walnuts.

Baklava is not at all difficult to prepare, as long as you treat the phyllo dough gently. Here are some tips:

1. *If using frozen dough, defrost it exactly as the package instructs. If the dough is at all frozen, the layers will stick together and tear.*
2. *Work with only about one-quarter of the dough at a time. Keep the remaining dough covered with a clean dish towel.*
3. *The melted butter between each layer of dough keeps the pastry light and flaky. Only a small amount of butter is needed for this, and it's not necessary to butter both sides of the sheet of dough, as long as there is butter between each layer.*
4. *When unrolled, each sheet of phyllo dough should fit into a 9- x 13-inch baking pan. If there is any excess dough, trim off and discard the excess. (You can cut off all the excess dough at once after you have finished assembling the Baklava.)*

2½ cups chopped walnuts
1½ cups semi-sweet chocolate, chopped
1 teaspoon cinnamon
1 8-ounce package Phyllo dough, defrosted if frozen
6 tablespoons butter, melted
1½ cups sugar
1 cup water
¼ cup honey

1. Preheat the oven to 350°F.
2. In a bowl, stir together the walnuts, chocolate, and cinnamon.
3. Remove about one-quarter of the phyllo dough and cover the remaining dough with a clean dish towel. Spray the bottom and sides of a 9- x 13-inch baking pan with baking spray, and lay one sheet of phyllo dough in the pan.

Yield: about 35 pieces of Baklava

Brush the sheet very lightly with melted butter. It is not necessary that every bit of the dough be covered with butter. Lay another sheet of dough over the first and brush with butter. Continue layering in this fashion until you have used approximately one-quarter of the dough.

4. Sprinkle the phyllo layers with approximately one-third of the chocolate-walnut filling. Repeat with another one-quarter of the phyllo dough and another one-third of the filling. Repeat again and cover the filling with the final one-quarter of phyllo dough.

5. Using a sharp knife, cut the Baklava into small squares or diamonds, a little larger than one-inch square.

6. Bake the Baklava for about 1 hour, or until it is golden brown.

7. In the meanwhile, prepare the honey syrup: Place the sugar, water, and honey in a saucepan. Bring to a boil, stirring to dissolve the sugar. Lower the heat and simmer gently for 20 minutes. Let cool.

8. As soon as the Baklava comes out of the oven, pour the honey syrup evenly over it. Transfer the pan to a rack to cool.

Cannoli

Is there anyone who has never sampled a cannoli—that deliciously crisp hollow tube of Italian pastry, filled with a luscious mixture of creamy ricotta cheese and chocolate chips? Cannoli makes an easy-to-prepare and memorable ending to any Italian dinner and is enjoyed by almost everyone. For chocolate lovers, these Cannoli—with a chocolate-ricotta filling—are even better than the traditional version.

Note: Cannoli shells may be purchased from specialty food stores. Also, to make the Cannoli even more festive, sprinkle colored crystallized sugar on each end of the pastries just before serving.

1 **15-ounce container ricotta cheese**
1 **cup confectioners' sugar**
2 **1-ounce squares unsweetened chocolate, melted**
½ **teaspoon vanilla**
¼ **cup mini semi-sweet chocolate chips**
8 **cannoli shells**
colored crystallized sugar, optional

Yield: 8 servings

1. In a large bowl, beat together the ricotta cheese, sugar, chocolate, and vanilla until well mixed. Stir in the chocolate chips. Refrigerate this mixture until shortly before serving the cannoli.

2. Using a spoon, fill the cannoli shells. If desired, sprinkle the cheese mixture that peeks out on each end with crystallized sugar. Refrigerate the cannoli until ready to serve.

Note: Cannoli are best eaten on the day they are made as the shells will begin to become soggy after a few hours.

Eclairs

*C*ertainly, no one needs an introduction to eclairs! But for anyone who dotes on these light, yet buttery pastries that are filled with custard and iced with chocolate glaze, Chocolate Eclairs take the cake—they are everything you always loved in an eclair, but now with a chocolate flavor.

PASTRY SHELLS
 1 recipe Chocolate Cream Puff Pastry from Profiteroles (page 32)

CUSTARD FILLING
 3 egg yolks
 ½ cup sugar
 2 tablespoons flour
 ⅔ cup boiling milk
 2 teaspoons butter
 ⅓ cup semi-sweet chocolate morsels

GLAZE
 1 recipe Chocolate Glaze from Boston Cream Pie (page 70)

Yield: 22 mini-eclairs

1. First make the pastry shells. Follow the recipe for the cream puff shells for making Profiteroles, except after you have dropped the pastry dough onto the baking sheet, with your fingertips, form it into oval shapes.
2. Make the filling: In a small saucepan, beat the egg yolks with the sugar, using a wire whisk, until the mixture is thick and pale. Beat in the flour. Add the boiling milk, beating as you add it.
3. Place the saucepan on the heat, and cook, stirring, until the mixture comes to a boil. Cook over a low heat, stirring, for 2 minutes longer. Remove the pan from the heat and stir in the butter and chocolate. Let sit, stirring occasionally, until the butter and chocolate are melted. Transfer the custard to a bowl, and cover with plastic wrap, placing the plastic directly on the custard to prevent a "skin" from forming. Refrigerate until chilled and firm.
4. Fill the bottom of each eclair shell with custard and place the top of the eclair shell over the custard. Spread with Chocolate Glaze.

Note: The Eclairs are best served at room temperature and can stay unrefrigerated for several hours. Leftovers should be stored in the refrigerator.

Profiteroles

*O*f all desserts, profiteroles are among my all-time favorites. For those unfamiliar with this delectable concoction, a profiterole starts with a cream puff shell, which is then filled with ice cream. Just before serving, hot fudge sauce is poured over the top.

Naturally, since I like profiteroles so much, I was eager to try making the cream puff shell from a chocolate dough, and I'm pleased to say that the results are spectacular! The puff itself tastes like an airy chocolate brownie, which makes a great contrast to the creamy ice cream and rich fudge sauce.

Note: Cream puff shells are quite easy to prepare, although the mixing of the dough takes a bit of old-fashioned "elbow grease." The trick to making crispy cream puffs is to remove any unbaked dough in the middle of the puffs as soon as the pastries emerge from the oven.

CHOCOLATE CREAM PUFF PASTRY
- 1 stick (½ cup) butter or margarine
- 1 cup water
- 1 cup flour
- 4 eggs
- ⅓ cup unsweetened cocoa powder
- ⅔ cup sugar

FILLING
- 1 quart chocolate ice cream, slightly softened
- 1 recipe Fudge Sauce from Fettuccine with Fudge Sauce (page 150)

Yield: 20 puffs or about 10 servings

1. Preheat the oven to 400°F.
2. Grease two large baking sheets.
3. In a heavy saucepan, heat the butter in the water. Cook until the butter melts. When the mixture comes to a boil, add the flour, all at once. Continue cooking, stirring vigorously, until the mixture forms a ball. This will take about 2 minutes.
4. Remove the saucepan from the heat. Add one egg to the mixture, and stir vigorously until the egg is completely incorporated. Beat in the cocoa and sugar. Now add the remaining eggs, one at a time, making certain that each is completely incorporated before beating in the next.
5. Drop the batter by heaping tablespoonsful onto the cookie sheet. Allow at least 1½ inches of space between the balls of batter because the dough will expand when baked.

6. Place the baking sheets in the oven and bake for 15 minutes. Lower the oven temperature to 350°F and bake for 20 minutes longer.

7. Remove the baking sheets from the oven. With a sharp knife, carefully make a slit, about 1 inch long, in the side of each puff to allow the steam to escape. Return the puffs to the oven and bake for 10 minutes longer.

8. Remove the baking sheets from the oven. Cut each puff in half crosswise. Using a fork, remove any unbaked dough from the inside of the puff. Reassemble each puff to form a sphere. Let cool on a rack.

9. When fully cooled, fill each puff with a scoop of ice cream. Freeze for several hours, or until ready to serve. To serve, place one or two puffs on each dessert plate and cover with a generous portion of Fudge Sauce.

Portuguese Almond "Cheesecakes"

QUEIJADINHAS DE AMÊNDOAS

*A*lthough these lovely morsels are called cheesecakes, they contain no cream cheese, milk, cream, or butter. In texture, they do somewhat resemble cheesecake, although, to my mind, they are more like ultra-rich brownies. Whatever you call them, these are wonderful offerings for a buffet dessert tray!

2 ¼ **cups sugar**
⅔ **cup water**
4 **ounces blanched almonds, finely ground**
⅔ **cup unsweetened cocoa powder**
3 **whole eggs**
9 **egg yolks**

Yield: 36 mini cakes

1. Place the sugar and water in a medium-sized, heavy saucepan. Bring to a boil, stirring often to dissolve the sugar.
2. Add the almonds and bring to a boil again.
3. Remove the pot from the heat. Add the cocoa and stir until dissolved.
4. In a large bowl, beat the eggs and egg yolks well. Gradually add to the pot, stirring constantly.
5. Preheat the oven to 300°F.
6. Place paper cups in mini-muffin tins. (You will need 36 tins. If you don't have this many, you will need to bake the cakes in batches.)
7. Place the pot on the stove over a very low heat. Cook, stirring frequently, until the mixture thickens. The texture will be like a somewhat runny pudding.
8. Fill the muffin tins nearly to the top.
9. Bake the cakes for 30 minutes. Remove from the tins and let cool. Chill until ready to serve.

Quesadillas

Quesa is the Spanish word for cheese, so we think of quesadillas as something (usually tortillas) filled with cheese. Quesadillas, however, can also be a Mexican dessert. Oddly enough, they don't contain cheese, but they do have the texture of cheesecake. These quesadillas, of course, are more like chocolate cheesecakes and are absolutely delicious.

4 eggs, separated
1 cup sugar
¾ cup cornstarch
⅓ cup unsweetened cocoa powder, sifted if lumpy
1 stick (½ cup) butter or margarine

Yield: 10 Quesadillas

1. Preheat the oven to 350°F.
2. Line muffin tins with paper muffin cups. (You will need about 10.)
3. In a large bowl, beat the egg whites until stiff and set aside.
4. In another large bowl, stir together the sugar, cornstarch, and cocoa. Using a pastry cutter, two knives, or your fingertips, cut in the butter until the mixture is crumbly. Beat in the egg yolks.
5. Stir about one-third of the beaten egg whites into the chocolate mixture to lighten the texture. Then fold in the rest of the egg whites gently but thoroughly.
6. Spoon the batter into the muffin tins, filling them almost to the top.
7. Bake the Quesadillas for about 30 minutes, or until a toothpick inserted in the center comes out clean. Remove the Quesadillas from the muffin tins and let cool on a rack. They may be served at room temperature or chilled.

Rugelach

*R*ugelach are made from a rich, cream cheese dough that is cut into small wedges and then rolled up with a filling that includes jam and cinnamon. Nuts and/or raisins are often added as well. Each rugelach makes a bite-size morsel that almost no one can refuse.

This recipe contains chocolate in the cream cheese pastry, which makes it even richer and more flavorful. Semi-sweet chocolate is also added to the filling.

DOUGH
- 1 stick (½ cup) butter or margarine, softened
- 1 3-ounce package cream cheese, softened
- ½ cup sugar
- 2 1-ounce squares unsweetened chocolate, melted
- 1 cup flour

FILLING
- 3 tablespoons jam (such as raspberry or apricot)
- 1 tablespoon sugar
- ½ teaspoon cinnamon
- 3 tablespoons finely chopped pecans
- 3 tablespoons finely ground semi-sweet chocolate

Yield: 36 Rugelach

1. In a large bowl, cream the butter and cream cheese with the sugar, continuing to beat until the sugar is fully incorporated. Beat in the chocolate, then the flour.
2. Divide the dough into 3 equal portions. Form each into a ball and then flatten to a thick disk. Wrap in plastic wrap and refrigerate for several hours or overnight.
3. Preheat the oven to 350°F.
4. Grease two large baking sheets.
5. On a lightly floured board, roll one of the dough disks into a circle about 8 inches in diameter. Spread 1 tablespoon of the jam around the outside of the circle. In a small bowl, stir together the sugar and cinnamon. Sprinkle the center portion of the circle that is not covered with jam with one-third of the cinnamon-sugar mixture (about 1 teaspoon). Sprinkle the part of the dough spread with jam with one-third of the pecans and one-third of the chocolate.
6. Using a pizza cutter or a sharp knife, divide the circle into 12 equal wedges. Beginning with the outer rim, roll up each wedge toward the center. Place the roll-up on the baking sheet. Repeat with the remaining wedges, so you have 12 roll-ups.
7. Repeat steps 5 and 6 with the two remaining disks of dough.
8. Bake the rugelach for about 20 minutes, or until lightly browned. Transfer to racks to cool.

Austrian Pastry Bars

This is one of the most buttery bars imaginable, with rich, dark chocolate pastry crust, topped with a toffee-like nut and chocolate chip mixture. The result is sensational!

RICH CHOCOLATE PASTRY CRUST
1 recipe Rich Chocolate Pastry Crust from German Sponge Tart (page 24)

FILLING
¾ **cup sliced almonds**
½ **cup sugar**
½ **teaspoon vinegar**
2 **tablespoons heavy or whipping cream**
4 **tablespoons butter**
½ **teaspoon vanilla**
½ **cup semi-sweet chocolate morsels**

Yield: 24 bars

1. Preheat the oven to 350°F.
2. Grease a 9- x 13-inch baking pan.
3. Make the pastry and press it into the bottom of the pan. Bake for 25 minutes.
4. While the pastry is baking, make the topping: Place the almonds in a large, ungreased skillet. Cook over a medium-high heat, stirring, until lightly browned. Immediately transfer the nuts to a plate so they don't continue to brown.
5. Place the sugar and vinegar in a small, heavy saucepan. Cook over a medium heat, stirring, until the sugar melts and then turns caramel colored. Remove from the heat and add the cream and butter. Stir until the butter melts and the mixture is smooth. Stir in the almonds and vanilla.
6. Spread the almond mixture in an even layer over the crust. (The layer will be very thin.) Sprinkle with the chocolate morsels. Return to the oven and bake for 15 minutes longer.
7. Transfer the pan to a rack to cool and then cut into bars.

Tiramisu

*T*here are as many variations of Tiramisu as there are Italian restaurants that serve it. The best Tiramisu layers sponge cakes that have been dipped in coffee syrup with a creamy custard containing mascarpone cheese. This is an Italian cream cheese that's about as different from American cream cheese as ricotta is from cottage cheese. Thus, there's no good substitute for mascarpone. Fortunately, since Tiramisu has become so popular, more and more cheese shops and specialty food stores now stock mascarpone.

Tiramisu requires several steps—none difficult, but they do take time. Chocolate Tiramisu, made with chocolate sponge wafers rather than store-bought cake, is even more time-consuming. But the results are well worth the effort; this is quite possibly the very best chocolate dessert I've ever experienced.

CHOCOLATE SPONGE WAFERS
  ½ **cup flour**
  3 **tablespoons unsweetened cocoa**
    powder, sifted
  4 **eggs, separated**
  ⅛ **teaspoon salt**
  1 **cup confectioners' sugar, divided**
  1 **teaspoon vanilla**

DIPPING SYRUP
  2 **tablespoons instant coffee granules**
  1 **cup water**
  ¼ **cup sugar**
  1 **teaspoon vanilla**
  1 **tablespoon sweet marsala**

1. First make the sponge wafers: Preheat the oven to 350°F.
2. Line two 11-inch x 16-inch baking sheets with waxed paper.
3. In a small bowl, stir together the flour and cocoa.
4. In a large bowl, beat the egg whites with the salt. Gradually beat in ½ cup confectioners' sugar. Continue beating until glossy.
5. In another bowl, beat the egg yolks. Gradually beat in the remaining ½ cup confectioners' sugar. Beat in the vanilla. Stir in the flour mixture. Stir in about one-quarter of the egg whites. Then fold in the rest gently.
6. Drop the batter, in oval shapes about 4 inches long by 1 inch wide, onto the prepared baking sheets. (The wafers will spread while baking.) Bake the wafers for 12 to 15 minutes, or until a toothpick inserted in the center of a wafer comes out clean. Let cool, then remove from the waxed paper. You will have about 20 wafers.
7. To make the dipping syrup, mix the coffee, water, and sugar in a small saucepan. Bring to a boil, stirring to

FILLING

8 egg yolks

½ cup plus 2 tablespoons sugar, divided

3 tablespoons sweet marsala

1 6-ounce package semi-sweet chocolate morsels

1 cup heavy or whipping cream

1 teaspoon vanilla

1 17-ounce container mascarpone cheese (about 2 cups)

1 tablespoon unsweetened cocoa powder

Yield: 12 servings

dissolve the coffee and sugar. Remove from the heat and stir in the vanilla and marsala. Set aside.

8. Prepare the filling: In the top of a double boiler (with simmering water in the bottom), place the egg yolks, ½ cup sugar, marsala, and chocolate. Heat, stirring constantly, until the chocolate melts. Transfer to a bowl and refrigerate until cool.

9. Beat the heavy cream with the 2 tablespoons sugar until whipped. Beat in the vanilla.

10. Beat the mascarpone cheese slightly. Beat in the chocolate custard mixture thoroughly. Fold in the whipped cream.

11. To assemble the Tiramisu, dip the chocolate wafers, one at a time, into the dipping syrup, letting them stay in the syrup for 2 to 3 seconds. As you dip the wafers, place them in the bottom of a 9- x 13-inch baking pan. After you have placed half the wafers in the pan, spread half the filling mixture over them. Repeat these layers.

12. Put the cocoa in a sifter and sift over the top of the Tiramisu. Cover with plastic wrap and let chill for several hours before serving.

Petits Fours

*P*etits Fours are little square cakes, only about as big as a single mouthful. Each pastry consists of two layers, usually made from yellow cake, put together with jam or another filling and then covered with icing, which is usually tinted a pale pastel shade. The cakes are often decorated with little sugar flowers.

Petits Fours are delightful little morsels, but Chocolate Petits Fours are truly marvelous treats. The cake layers are dense chocolate, the filling rich and buttery chocolate, and the icing a deep dark chocolate. These make an elegant dessert, whatever the occasion.

CAKE
- **2 eggs**
- **2 cups sugar**
- **1 stick (½ cup) butter or margarine, melted**
- **2 cups flour**
- **¾ cup unsweetened cocoa powder, sifted if lumpy**
- **2 teaspoons baking powder**
- **⅛ teaspoon salt**
- **⅔ cup boiling water**

FILLING
- **½ stick (4 tablespoons) butter or margarine, softened**
- **3 1-ounce squares unsweetened chocolate, melted**
- **2 cups confectioners' sugar**
- **3 tablespoons heavy or whipping cream**

ICING
- **2 cups (1 pint) minus 3 tablespoons heavy or whipping cream**
- **2 cups semi-sweet chocolate morsels**
- **candied violets or other edible flowers, optional (or sprinkle with colored crystallized sugar, such as red and green for Christmas)**

1. First make the cake layers: Preheat the oven to 350°F.
2. Line a 9- x 13-inch baking pan with waxed paper and grease the paper.
3. In a large bowl, beat the eggs. Gradually beat in the sugar, continuing to beat until the mixture is thick and pale yellow. Beat in the melted butter.
4. In another bowl, stir together the flour, cocoa, baking powder, and salt. Add to the egg mixture, beating or stirring until the dry ingredients are incorporated. Stir in the water.
5. Pour the batter into the prepared pan. Bake the cake for 30 to 35 minutes, or until a toothpick inserted in the center comes out clean. Transfer the pan to a rack to cool. When completely cool, tip the cake out of the pan and remove the waxed paper.
6. With a sharp knife, carefully cut the cake in half horizontally, so you now have two very thin 9- x 13-inch layers. Place the bottom layer, cut side up, on a large plate or baking pan.
7. Make the filling: Beat together the butter, chocolate, confectioners' sugar, and heavy cream until the mixture is smooth. Spread on the bottom layer. Cover with the top

Yield: 70 Petits Fours

cake layer, cut side down. Place the cake in the refrigerator and chill well for at least 2 hours.

8. Cut the cake into cubes, about $1\frac{1}{4}$ inches in size. You will get about 10 cuts along the long side of the cake and 7 cuts along the short side, so you will have about 70 cubes.

9. Make the icing: Heat the cream to boiling. Remove the pan from the heat and stir in the chocolate. Let cool, stirring occasionally, until the mixture is thick. This will take 5 to 8 minutes. Carefully, pick up the cake squares, one at a time, and coat the top and sides with the icing. Place the squares on a platter or in small paper cups. Decorate each square with a candied flower or crystallized sugar, if desired.

Icebox Cake

*T*his dessert is so easy to assemble, even a child could make it. In fact, when I was only about eleven years old, I started making it regularly whenever my parents entertained. Icebox Cake consists of freshly whipped cream, layered with chocolate wafers. After sitting in the "icebox" for several hours, the wafers absorb liquid from the whipped cream and become cakelike.

This dessert is so universally well liked and easy to prepare, it's unfortunate that it's far less popular today than it was in the fifties. If you're interested in reviving Icebox Cake, I suggest you try this new chocolate version, which is as rich as the original but uses chocolate whipped cream to impart even more flavor.

1 pint heavy or whipping cream
¼ cup unsweetened cocoa powder
⅓ cup sugar
1 teaspoon vanilla
1 9-ounce package Nabisco Famous Chocolate Wafers

Yield: 12 servings

1. In a large bowl, stir together the heavy cream, cocoa, and sugar. Beat until whipped and thick. Beat in the vanilla.
2. Remove 3 chocolate wafers and crush them. Reserve.
3. Sandwich the remaining chocolate wafers together with the whipped cream, using about 1½ tablespoons of cream between the wafers. After you have put together three or four cookies, place them on their sides on a flat platter, at least 17 inches long. Keep adding cookies, making a long roll, which will be about 15 inches long when finished. Use the remaining whipped cream to frost the top and sides of the roll. Sprinkle with the reserved cookie crumbs.
4. Cover the Icebox Cake with plastic wrap and chill several hours before serving. To serve the cake, cut slices on the diagonal.

FRUIT
and
CHOCOLATE:

*What a
Combination!*

Grunt with Blueberries

*G*runts, cobblers, and roly-polys are all names of early American fruit desserts that also contained biscuit dough. With a cobbler, the dough is dropped over the fruit and then baked, with the result looking like old cobblestone streets. A roly-poly is similar to a jelly roll. But no one is quite certain how the name grunt originated. Some say that the dough makes a grunting sort of sound as it simmers in the skillet. But while my skillet whistles as the steam escapes, it never grunts. Perhaps grunt refers to the sounds of pleasure emitted by people who eat the dessert; my husband most definitely expressed his satisfaction with numerous sorts of noises.

This recipe is for a blueberry grunt, and the biscuit dough is chocolate flavored. The taste is like a warm chocolate cake, covered with blueberries in syrup.

The grunt should be served warm, within about 2 hours of cooking it. Fortunately, the dessert takes only about 10 minutes to prepare (and 45 minutes to cook), so it's an easy choice for the last-minute cook.

BLUEBERRY MIXTURE
- **2 pints fresh blueberries, rinsed and picked over**
- **¾ cup sugar**
- **¼ cup water**
- **1 tablespoon lemon juice**

DOUGH
- **1 cup flour**
- **¼ cup unsweetened cocoa powder, sifted if lumpy**
- **⅓ cup sugar**
- **½ teaspoon baking soda**
- **⅛ teaspoon salt**
- **3 tablespoons butter or margarine, melted**
- **⅔ cup buttermilk (or place 2 teaspoons vinegar in a measuring cup and add milk to the ⅔-cup mark)**

Yield: 6 to 8 servings

1. Place the blueberries, sugar, water, and lemon juice in a large skillet with a tight-fitting lid. Stir well. Bring the ingredients to a boil over a low heat.

2. Meanwhile, in a bowl, stir together the flour, cocoa, sugar, baking soda, and salt. Add the melted butter and buttermilk, and stir just until the dry ingredients are moistened.

3. Drop the dough by large tablespoonfuls onto the simmering blueberry mixture. (You will make 8 to 10 large balls of dough.)

4. Cover the skillet and simmer over a low heat, about 45 minutes. A toothpick inserted into the biscuits will come out clean, and they will not be sticky to the touch.

5. To serve, place a biscuit on a serving plate and cover with blueberry syrup. Serve with ice cream or whipped cream, if desired.

Apple Brown Betty

Everyone loves Apple Brown Betty, warm and fragrant from the oven, especially when topped with a scoop of vanilla ice cream. This is the type of homey American dessert that satisfies the soul as well as the stomach. It's also a very simple dessert to make: Fresh apple slices are layered with a sweet, spicy bread crumb mixture and then baked until the apples are tender and the crumbs form a luscious, browned crust.

In this version, chocolate chips are scattered among the apple slices and the crumb mixture is flavored with cocoa. The result is the best Apple Brown Betty you've ever tasted!

CRUMB MIXTURE
  2 cups soft fresh bread crumbs, made from high quality white bread
  ⅓ cup brown sugar, preferably dark brown
  ⅓ cup sugar
  ⅓ cup unsweetened cocoa powder
  1 teaspoon cinnamon

FILLING
  6 medium apples, peeled, cored, and cut into ½-inch slices
  ½ cup semi-sweet chocolate morsels
  ⅓ cup water
  3 tablespoons butter or margarine, cut into small pieces

Yield: 8 servings

1. In a bowl, stir together all the ingredients for the crumb mixture.
2. Preheat the oven to 375°F.
3. Grease an 8-inch-square baking pan.
4. Sprinkle 2 tablespoons of the crumb mixture evenly on the bottom of the pan. Spread half the apple slices on top and sprinkle with half the chocolate. Pour the water over the top.
5. Sprinkle about one-third of the remaining crumb mixture in the pan and sprinkle on about half the butter. Cover with the remaining apples and remaining chocolate, followed by the remaining crumb mixture and remaining butter.
6. Bake for about 35 minutes, or until the apples are tender and the topping crisp and browned. Transfer the pan to a rack to cool. This dessert is best served warm or at room temperature.

Apple Roly-Poly

*L*ike cobblers and grunts, roly-polys are another early American dessert made with biscuit dough and fruit. Here the dough is rolled up, jelly-roll style, around the filling—which may contain jam, as well as fruit—before being baked. This chocolate roly-poly starts with a rich chocolate biscuit dough and is filled with a mixture of chopped apples, semi-sweet chocolate, and jam. It's wonderful on its own or with whipped cream or ice cream.

FILLING
  ⅓ **cup apricot or seedless raspberry jam**
  ⅓ **cup finely chopped semi-sweet chocolate**
  1 **apple, peeled, cored, and finely chopped**

DOUGH
  2 **cups flour**
  ⅓ **cup unsweetened cocoa powder, sifted if lumpy**
  ¾ **cup sugar**
  1 **teaspoon baking soda**
  1 **teaspoon baking powder**
  ⅛ **teaspoon salt**
  3 **tablespoons butter or margarine**
  1 **egg, beaten**
  ⅔ **cup plain yogurt**
  1 **teaspoon vanilla**

  Yield: 12 servings

1. In a small bowl, stir together the jam, chocolate, and apple. Set aside.
2. Preheat the oven to 350°F.
3. Grease a baking sheet.
4. In a large bowl, stir together the flour, cocoa, sugar, baking soda, baking powder, and salt. With your fingertips, a pastry cutter, or two knives, cut in the butter until the mixture resembles coarse meal.
5. In a small bowl, stir together the egg, yogurt, and vanilla. Add to the flour mixture and stir until a dough forms.
6. Turn the dough out onto a well-floured board or cloth and, using a well-floured rolling pin, roll out to a 15- by 8-inch rectangle. The dough will be quite moist. Spread the apple mixture evenly over the dough, leaving a 1-inch border on all sides.
7. Beginning with a long side, roll up the dough, jelly-roll fashion. Since the dough is quite sticky, the easiest way to do this is to flour a knife and use the knife to help pry the dough off the board and guide in the rolling. When completely rolled up, rest the baking sheet on top of the roll. Then reverse the sheet and the roll, so the baking sheet now rests on the countertop. Gently remove the board. If there are any holes in the top of the roll, patch them up.

New Chocolate Classics

8. Bake the roly-poly for 30 minutes. Because the dough is soft (not like a bread dough), the roly-poly will spread and flatten as it bakes. Transfer the baking sheet to a rack to cool. The roly-poly may be served warm or at room temperature.

Clafoutis

A Clafoutis is a baked French pancake that's light and airy and generally contains fruit, most often cherries. The pancake puffs as it bakes and then falls as it cools. Thus, it is best served hot from the oven or warm. Clafoutis is one of the easiest of all desserts to prepare and is virtually foolproof.

This Chocolate Clafouti is dark, without being overly rich and has a wonderful custardy texture.

1 cup milk
¾ cup sugar
3 eggs
1 tablespoon vanilla
⅛ teaspoon salt
¼ cup flour
¼ cup unsweetened cocoa powder
1 1-pound can pitted bing cherries, drained well
⅓ cup semi-sweet chocolate morsels
whipped cream or vanilla ice cream, optional

Yield: 6 servings

1. Place the milk, sugar, eggs, vanilla, salt, flour, and cocoa in a blender or food processor and process until smooth. Chill this mixture for at least an hour.
2. Preheat the oven to 350°F.
3. Spray a 10-inch ovenproof skillet with cooking oil spray and heat for a couple of minutes over medium heat. Stir the Clafoutis batter well and pour enough batter into the skillet to reach a height of about ¼ inch. Cook over a medium heat until the batter pulls away from the sides and begins to set. (Part of the batter will remain runny.)
4. Remove the skillet from the heat and distribute the cherries and chocolate morsels evenly over the top. Pour the remaining batter over them.
5. Place the skillet in the oven and bake for about 45 minutes, or until the Clafoutis is set. Transfer the skillet to a rack, and cut the Clafoutis into wedges to serve. Serve with whipped cream or ice cream, if desired.

Ambrosia

*A*mbrosia is defined as "food of the Gods." Although no one has ever said exactly what this food might be, the most basic elements of recipes for Ambrosia start with sliced oranges, confectioners' sugar, and shredded coconut. Whipped cream is often added, as is crushed pineapple. Although I've never seen it previously, certainly no "God" could possibly object to the enhancement of Ambrosia with cocoa.

2 oranges
1 cup shredded coconut
1 cup heavy or whipping cream
¾ cup confectioners' sugar
¼ cup unsweetened cocoa powder, sifted
    if lumpy

Yield: 4 to 6 servings

1. Peel the oranges. Cut off the tough inner membrane covering the outside of the peeled orange. Cut the oranges into slices about ¼ inch thick. Toss with the coconut.

2. In a large bowl, beat the cream until thick. Beat in the confectioners' sugar and cocoa, continuing to beat until the mixture has the consistency of whipped cream. Gently fold in the orange-coconut mixture. Serve immediately.

Strawberry Shortcake with Chocolate-Covered Strawberries

*T*his is a dream dessert—the classic strawberry shortcake, but with everything in chocolate: a rich chocolate shortcake, filled with strawberries and chocolate whipped cream. As a final touch, the cake is decorated with luscious chocolate-covered strawberries. This is one of the most wonderful springtime desserts immaginable!

CHOCOLATE SHORTBREAD
  2 cups flour
  ⅔ cup sugar plus 1 tablespoon sugar, divided
  ⅓ cup unsweetened cocoa powder, sifted if lumpy
  1 tablespoon baking powder
  1½ cups heavy cream or whipping cream
  up to 2 tablespoons milk, if needed

STRAWBERRY FILLING
  2 12-ounce containers strawberries
  3 tablespoons sugar

CHOCOLATE WHIPPED CREAM
  1½ cups heavy cream or whipping cream
  ⅓ cup sugar
  3 tablespoons unsweetened cocoa powder

Yield: 8 generous servings

1. Preheat the oven to 375°F.
2. Grease and flour a 9-inch-round cake pan.
3. In a large bowl, stir together the flour, ⅔ cup sugar, cocoa, and baking powder. Stir in the heavy cream, mixing with a spoon until the dry ingredients are moistened. If the mixture is too dry, add up to 2 tablespoons milk.
4. Spoon the dough into the prepared pan, and flatten it with your hands into an even layer. Sprinkle with the remaining 1 tablespoon sugar.
5. Bake the shortbread for 30 minutes, or until a toothpick inserted in the center comes out clean. Transfer to a rack to cool. When completely cool, remove from the pan, and cut in half horizontally.
6. Meanwhile, reserve 8 perfect strawberries. Hull the rest, and cut into thin slices. Toss with the 3 tablespoons sugar. Let sit in the refrigerator until ready to assemble the cake.
7. At least an hour before serving the cake, mix together the ingredients for the whipped cream. Place in the refrigerator to dissolve the cocoa.
8. At any time on the day you are serving the dessert, prepare the chocolate-covered strawberries. (Let sit at room temperature until ready to serve.)
9. Shortly before serving the dessert, place the bottom cake layer, cut side up, on a serving plate. Cover with the

strawberries, including any liquid that formed in the bowl.

10. Whip the chocolate-flavored cream until stiff. Spread the bottom cake layer with a little more than half the whipped cream. Cover with the top cake layer, cut side down. Press down slightly. Form the remaining whipped cream into 8 large dollops on top of the cake. Place a chocolate-covered strawberry in the center of each dollop. Serve immediately.

CHOCOLATE-COVERED STRAWBERRIES
8 perfect strawberries
4 ounces semi-sweet chocolate

1. Leave the hulls on the berries. Wash them quickly and place on several layers of paper towels. Let sit for at least 1 hour, or until completely dry.

2. Line a baking pan or tray with waxed paper.

3. Melt the chocolate in the top of a double boiler. When melted, dip each berry, nearly to the hull, in the melted chocolate. Place on the waxed paper. When all the berries have been coated, place the pan in the refrigerator only long enough to set the chocolate. Transfer the berries from the paper to a plate and let sit at room temperature until ready to place on the shortcake.

Apricot Fool

ruit fools are an early American dessert (going back to when "fool" was a term of endearment). Fruit fools contain pureed fruit and whipped cream. The result is a rich, creamy dessert with a mousse-like quality. This version adds cocoa and chocolate liqueur to the fool, which makes a lovely contrast to the pureed apricots.

8 ounces dried apricots (about 1½ cups)
2⅓ cups water
¾ cup sugar
¼ cup crème de cacao
1 cup heavy or whipping cream
2 tablespoons unsweetened cocoa powder

Yield: 6 to 8 servings

1. Place the apricots, water, and sugar in a heavy saucepan. Bring to a boil. Lower the heat and simmer, covered, for 10 minutes. Let cool, then puree the apricots and cooking liquid in a food processor. Stir in the crème de cacao and chill.

2. Meanwhile, place the cream and cocoa in a mixing bowl. Stir well to dissolve the cocoa. Chill for at least 1 hour. Then whip the cream until soft peaks form. Fold the whipped cream into the apricot mixture and chill well.

3. Serve the fool in dessert bowls.

TOTALLY
DECADENT
PUDDINGS

Indian Pudding

*I*ndian Pudding is a traditional New England dessert, a slow-baked mixture that's flavored with cornmeal, spices, and molasses. Some people (particularly those who come from Boston, like me) love this pudding, while others are quite indifferent to it. But if this is a favored dessert, you are certain to love chocolate Indian Pudding as much or more than the original.

3½ **cups milk, divided**
½ **cup yellow cornmeal**
3 **1-ounce squares unsweetened chocolate**
2 **tablespoons butter or margarine**
¼ **cup molasses**
¾ **cup sugar**
1 **teaspoon cinnamon**
1 **teaspoon ginger**
½ **teaspoon nutmeg**
⅛ **teaspoon salt**
⅛ **teaspoon baking soda**
1 **egg, beaten**

Yield: 8 servings

1. Preheat the oven to 275°F.
2. Grease a 2-quart-round casserole dish.
3. Place 3 cups of milk in a large heavy pot, and bring to a boil. Meanwhile, dissolve the cornmeal in the remaining ½ cup milk. When the milk has come to a boil, add the cornmeal mixture, stirring constantly. Cook the mixture at a very gentle boil, stirring frequently, for 15 minutes.
4. Remove the pot from the heat, and add the chocolate and butter. Stir until melted. Stir in the molasses, sugar, cinnamon, ginger, nutmeg, salt, and baking soda. Mix well. Beat in the egg.
5. Pour the mixture into the prepared dish. Bake the pudding until set, 1¾ to 2 hours. Serve warm or chilled.

Rice Pudding

A well-made rice pudding is one of the most satisfying desserts imaginable. With its simplicity of ingredients, rice pudding brings back memories of our childhood, when familiar flavors were the most comforting. Chocolate Rice Pudding has an extra creaminess, with chocolate adding a deliciously rich taste. Serve it plain or with whipped cream.

4 cups water
¼ teaspoon salt
1 cup raw rice
3 cups milk
3 1-ounce squares unsweetened chocolate, melted
1 ¼ cups sugar
1 teaspoon vanilla

Yield: 8 to 10 servings

1. In a large, heavy saucepan, bring the water and salt to a boil. Stir in the rice. Reduce the heat to a very low setting and cook the rice, uncovered, for 35 minutes. Pour the rice into a strainer to drain off any excess water and return the rice to the saucepan.

2. Add the milk, chocolate, and sugar. Simmer the rice, uncovered, keeping it at a very gentle boil, until most of the liquid has been absorbed, about 40 minutes. Stir occasionally at first, but when the liquid is nearly gone, stir often.

3. Remove the rice from the heat and stir in the vanilla. Transfer the pudding to a serving bowl. Let it cool to room temperature, then chill well before serving.

Tapioca Pudding

A childhood favorite, but now in dark, rich chocolate. This is a snap to make—almost as easy as pudding from a box, yet so much better!

3 tablespoons quick-cooking tapioca
¾ cup sugar
1 egg, beaten
2 1-ounce squares unsweetened
    chocolate, melted
2 cups milk
1 tablespoon butter or margarine

Yield: 4 servings

1. Place all the ingredients in the top of a double boiler. Cook over boiling water, stirring occasionally, for about 20 minutes. The mixture will be smooth but still quite liquidy. It will become firmer and puddinglike in texture as it cools.

2. Pour the pudding into a serving bowl. As it is cooling to room temperature, stir once or twice to distribute the tapioca evenly. When the bowl reaches room temperature, chill the tapioca.

Noodle Pudding

*A*nyone who's ever eaten in a New York deli or had a traditional Jewish meal is likely to have experienced the wonderful taste of a sweet noodle pudding, generally served warm with the meal. This version—made richer and sweeter with the addition of chocolate and extra sugar—is so delicious, it's better served as a dessert than as a dinner accompaniment.

8 ounces wide egg noodles
3 1-ounce squares unsweetened
    chocolate, melted
2 tablespoons butter or margarine
8 ounces small curd cottage cheese
½ pint sour cream
3 eggs, beaten
1 cup sugar

Yield: 10 to 12 servings

1. Preheat the oven to 350°F.
2. Grease a 9-inch-square baking pan.
3. Bring a large pot of salted water to a boil. Add the noodles and cook until they are just tender, about 6 minutes. Drain and return the noodles to the hot pot. Add the chocolate and butter and stir until melted.
4. Meanwhile, in a large bowl, beat together the cottage cheese, sour cream, eggs, and sugar. Add the noodle mixture and stir well.
5. Spread the noodle mixture in the prepared pan. Bake for 15 minutes. Lower the oven temperature to 300°F and bake for 1 hour longer. Let the pudding cool on a rack and chill before serving.

Oeufs à la Neige

*O*eufs à la Neige is a classic French dessert that translates into "snow eggs" and consists of large ovals of poached meringue nestled in a delicate custard sauce. Although the chocolate added to this recipe results in "eggs" that appear to have been made from dirty, rather than pristine, snow, the rich chocolate flavor more than compensates for the lack of whiteness.

CUSTARD SAUCE

⅔ cup semi-sweet chocolate morsels
2½ cups milk
2 eggs
⅓ cup sugar
1 teaspoon vanilla

MERINGUES

1 cup milk
4 egg whites
½ cup sugar
2 tablespoons unsweetened cocoa powder
½ teaspoon vanilla

Yield: 6 servings

1. First make the custard: In a heavy saucepan, melt the chocolate in the milk, and continue heating until the milk comes to a simmer.

2. In a bowl, thoroughly beat the eggs with the sugar. Add about ½ cup of the hot milk mixture to the eggs, and beat well. Add the egg mixture to the saucepan. Cook over low heat, stirring constantly, until the mixture thickens slightly. Do not let it come to a boil. This is a custard *sauce,* so it will be less thick than a puddinglike custard.

3. Remove the pan from the heat and stir in the vanilla. Transfer the contents of the pan to a bowl. Cover with plastic wrap, so the plastic rests on the sauce. (This prevents a "skin" from forming on the custard.) Chill until cold.

4. Meanwhile, make the meringues: Place the milk in a large pot, and add enough water to make about 2 inches of liquid in the pot. Bring to a simmer.

5. As you are waiting for the liquid to heat up, in a large bowl, beat the egg whites until soft peaks form. Gradually beat in the sugar, continuing to beat until the mixture is thick and glossy. Beat in the cocoa and vanilla.

6. Using two large spoons that have been dipped in cold water, form the meringue into about 6 large ovals. As you form each oval, drop it into the simmering liquid. Do not let the liquid come to a boil. The ovals shouldn't be

crowded in the pot, so you will need to cook them in two batches. Simmer the ovals for about 8 minutes. Then turn them over and simmer for another 4 minutes. Remove the ovals from the liquid with a slotted spoon and transfer to a plate lined with paper towels. Let cool slightly.

7. Pour the custard sauce into a large shallow serving bowl. Gently drop in the meringue "eggs." Cover the bowl and chill until ready to serve.

Floating Island

*T*his dessert, also known by the French term Ile Flotie, looks like an impressive meringue "island," surrounded by a sea of custard. In this version, both the island and "sea" are chocolate, and the result is the most hedonistically pleasurable dessert. The meringue softly dissolves in your mouth, while the custard provides a rich and creamy contrast.

MERINGUES
1½ cups egg whites (10 to 12)
½ teaspoon cream of tartar
1⅔ cups sugar
⅓ cup unsweetend cocoa powder

CUSTARD SAUCE
1 recipe Custard Sauce from Oeufs à la Neige (page 58)

Yield: 8 to 10 servings

1. Preheat the oven to 350°F.
2. Grease a tube pan.
3. In a large bowl, beat the egg whites with the cream of tartar until stiff. Gradually beat in the sugar, continuing to beat until the mixture is thick and glossy. Beat in the cocoa.
4. Turn the mixture into the prepared pan. Cover loosely with foil. (Just lay the foil on top of the pan; don't crimp the edges.) Place the pan in a larger pan of hot water. Place in the oven and bake for 30 minutes.
5. Transfer the pan to a rack to cool. Then chill for several hours. Do not unmold until ready to serve.
6. Prepare the custard sauce according to the recipe for Oeufs à la Neige.
7. Just before serving, tip the meringue out onto a large plate. Surround with some of the custard sauce, and serve the remaining sauce separately, spooning some over each serving.

Mexican Baked Custard

JIRICALLA

This traditional baked vanilla custard relies on cornmeal, rather than flour, for thickening. The result is a lovely texture, with very little flavor of the cornmeal. The custard is covered with a meringue, which is then baked until set and browned. Chocolate Jiricalla is a perfect dessert to follow a Mexican-style meal.

2 cups milk
2 tablespoons butter or margarine
3 1-ounce squares unsweetened chocolate
1¼ cups sugar, divided
⅛ teaspoon salt
¼ teaspoon cinnamon
⅛ teaspoon nutmeg
¼ cup yellow cornmeal, mixed with ¼ cup water
3 eggs, separated
½ teaspoon vanilla
2 tablespoons unsweetened cocoa powder

Yield: 6 to 8 servings

1. Grease a 1½- to 2-quart baking dish.
2. In a large, heavy saucepan, combine the milk, butter, chocolate, 1 cup sugar, salt, cinnamon, nutmeg, and cornmeal mixture. Cook over a medium heat, stirring, until the butter and chocolate have melted.
3. Using a wire whisk, beat the egg yolks in a small bowl. Gradually beat in about ¾ cup of the hot milk mixture. Add the contents of the bowl to the saucepan and cook over low heat until it reaches a custardlike consistency. (It will be a fairly thin custard.) Do not let the mixture boil at any time. Stir in the vanilla.
4. Pour the custard into the prepared baking dish. Let cool, stirring occasionally, for about 10 minutes.
5. Meanwhile, preheat the oven to 350°F.
6. In a large bowl, beat the egg whites until stiff. Gradually beat in the remaining ¼ cup sugar, continuing to beat until the egg whites are glossy. Beat in the cocoa powder.
7. Drop large spoonfuls of the meringue over the top of the custard. Using a knife, gently spread the meringue so it covers the custard in an even layer.
8. Bake the custard for about 12 minutes, or until the meringue is set.
9. Transfer the baking pan to a rack to cool. When it has cooled to room temperature, refrigerate the custard until very cold.

Creme Caramel

*T*his is a classic Spanish flan that's so delicate and elegant, it's served at many fine restaurants, even those that aren't Spanish. Creme Caramel consists of a custard that's baked in a dish that has first been lined with caramelized sugar. As the flan bakes, the caramel flavor permeates the custard, and the sugar also dissolves to form a lovely thick sauce for the finished dessert.

The chocolate version of Creme Caramel is as rich and delicate as the original, but with a wonderful brownie-like flavor.

CARAMEL
1½ cups sugar
¼ cup water

CUSTARD
3 cups milk
3 1-ounce squares unsweetened chocolate
1½ cups sugar
3 whole eggs
6 egg yolks
1 teaspoon vanilla

Yield: 8 to 10 servings

1. First make the caramel: In a heavy saucepan, cook the sugar and water, stirring until the sugar dissolves. Bring to a boil and let cook, swirling the pan occasionally, until the mixture is a lovely amber color. The darker the color, the more flavorful the caramel. But if it becomes too dark, it will taste burnt. So it's better to have it a little on the light side than overcooked.

2. Immediately pour the caramel syrup into a 1½- to 2-quart-round casserole dish. Swirl the dish so the caramel coats the sides as well as the bottom. Set the dish aside.

3. Preheat the oven to 325°F.

4. In a saucepan, heat the milk and chocolate until the chocolate has melted and the milk reaches the simmering point. Do not let it boil.

5. Meanwhile, in a large bowl, using a wire whisk, beat the sugar with the whole eggs and egg yolks very well. Gradually whisk in the hot milk mixture, beating the whole time. Stir in the vanilla.

6. Place the caramel-lined dish in a large roasting or baking pan. Pour the custard mixture into the dish. Then fill the pan with hot water to come about halfway up the sides of the casserole dish.

7. Bake the custard for about 1½ hours, or until set. Let cool on a rack, then chill well.
8. Just before serving, run a knife around the edges of the custard and invert onto a serving plate. The caramel syrup will form a sauce over the upside-down custard. Any syrup remaining in the dish should be spooned out over the custard.

Diplomat Pudding

*T*his is a spectacularly delicious dessert that's a cross between a bread pudding (made with cake and macaroons instead of bread) and a baked custard. Diplomat Pudding is generally vanilla with a slight almond flavoring: vanilla cake layers, almond amaretti, and vanilla custard. This version is darkly chocolate and even more wonderful.

Note: This recipe calls for 1 cup coarsely chopped amaretti (Italian almond macaroons found in specialty food stores). My recipe for Chocolate Amaretti appears on page 110. Using a few of these makes the best Diplomat Pudding, but if you would prefer to purchase commercial amaretti, the dessert will still be delicious.

SPONGE CAKE
- 2 eggs, separated
- ⅓ cup sugar
- 2 tablespoons water
- ¼ cup unsweetened cocoa powder, sifted if lumpy
- ½ teaspoon vanilla
- 2 tablespoons flour
- 2 tablespoons cornstarch

PUDDING
- ¼ cup dried cherries
- 2 tablespoons candied orange rind
- 3 tablespoons crème de cacao
- 1 cup coarsely chopped amaretti (see Note)
- 5 whole eggs
- 2 egg yolks
- 1½ cups sugar
- ½ teaspoon grated orange rind
- 3 1-ounce squares unsweetened chocolate, melted
- 4 cups milk

1. Make the sponge cake: Preheat the oven to 350°F.
2. Grease and flour a 9- x 5-inch loaf pan.
3. In a small bowl, beat the egg whites until stiff. Set aside.
4. In another bowl, beat the egg yolks. Beat in the sugar thoroughly. Beat in the water, cocoa, and vanilla. Stir in the flour and cornstarch. Stir about half the egg whites into the batter to lighten it. Then fold in the rest gently but thoroughly.
5. Spread the batter evenly in the prepared pan. (The batter will be only about an inch high.) Bake the cake for about 20 minutes, or until a toothpick inserted in the center of the cake comes out clean.
6. Transfer the pan to a rack to cool. When cool, remove the cake from the pan and cut it into ¼-inch-thick slices.
7. Make the pudding: In a small bowl, stir together the cherries, candied orange, and crème de cacao. Let sit for 15 minutes.
8. Preheat the oven to 325°F.
9. Grease a 2-quart-round casserole dish.

10. Use half the cake slices to cover the bottom of the casserole dish. Sprinkle with half the amaretti, then half the fruit/liqueur mixture. Repeat these layers.

11. In a large bowl, beat the eggs and the egg yolks. Gradually beat in the sugar. When the mixture is thick and pale, beat in the orange rind and melted chocolate. Stir in the milk. Pour over the cake mixture in the casserole dish.

12. Place the casserole dish in a pan of hot water and place in the oven. Bake for about 1 hour, 20 minutes, or until the pudding is set and a toothpick inserted in the center comes out clean.

13. Transfer the pudding to a rack to cool and chill before serving.

Zuppa Inglese

*Z*uppa Inglese translates into "English soup" and is the Italian version of trifle, an English dessert that layers sponge or pound cake, alcohol, and custard for a highly festive treat. Chocolate Zuppa Inglese starts with a chocolate pound cake, which is moistened with a potent mixture of rum and chocolate liqueur, and layered with a rich chocolate custard. It's definitely a dessert for adults only!

Note: This recipe calls for half a French Pound Cake. Make the entire cake, use half for the Zuppa Inglese, and enjoy the rest of the cake.

½ **French Pound Cake (page 89)**
3 **egg yolks**
⅔ **cup confectioners' sugar**
3 **tablespoons unsweetened cocoa powder**
3 **tablespoons flour**
2 **cups milk, scalded**
5 **tablespoons crème de cacao**
¼ **cup dark rum**

Yield: 10 servings

1. Slice the pound cake into ¼-inch slices.
2. In the top of a double boiler (off the heat), beat together the egg yolks and confectioners' sugar. Beat in the cocoa and flour. Add the hot milk gradually, beating constantly.
3. Place the pot over boiling water. Cook, stirring, for about 5 minutes, or until the mixture becomes custardlike. Do not let it boil. Remove from the heat, and stir as it is cooling.
4. In a small bowl, stir together the crème de cacao and rum.
5. Place one-quarter of the cake slices in an attractive serving bowl, cutting the pieces so they completely cover the bottom of the bowl. Sprinkle the cake with one-third of the rum mixture and cover with one-third of the custard. Press down slightly to release any air bubbles. Repeat these layers twice more. Place the remaining one-quarter of the cake slices on the top.
6. Cover the bowl and chill for several hours before serving. Serve alone or accompanied by whipped cream or chocolate whipped cream (see Strawberry Shortcake, page 50).

CAKES
NEVER HAD IT
SO GOOD

Angel Food Cake

*A*ngel food cakes have become increasingly popular of late due to their nonexistent fat content (they contain no butter, oil, or egg yolks). Chocolate Angel Food cake is just as heart-healthy as its white counterpart, but the cocoa has the effect of making the cake seem quite rich, indeed.

Note: This cake calls for 13 egg whites. If you wish, you may accumulate the whites gradually in a container in the freezer and defrost them when you have enough egg whites to make this cake.

1 cup minus 2 tablespoons flour
⅓ cup unsweetened cocoa powder, sifted if lumpy
⅓ cup plus 1¼ cups sugar, divided
13 egg whites (about 1⅔ cups)
1¼ teaspoons cream of tartar
1 teaspoon vanilla

Yield: 10 to 12 servings

1. Preheat the oven to 350°F.
2. In a bowl, stir together the flour, cocoa, and ⅓ cup sugar.
3. In a large bowl, beat the egg whites until foamy. Add the cream of tartar and continue beating until the whites are stiff. Gradually beat in the 1¼ cups sugar. When done, the mixture will be very glossy. Beat in the vanilla. Stir in the dry ingredients, mixing them gently by hand, so they are incorporated, but the egg whites do not deflate.
4. Turn the batter into a deep *ungreased* tube pan.
5. Bake the cake for 45 minutes, or until a toothpick inserted in the deepest part of the cake comes out clean. When the cake is done, let it cool upside down on a cake rack. When fully cool, remove the cake from the pan.

Gingerbread

*E*veryone's had gingerbread, and virtually everyone loves it. But how many people have ever tasted chocolate gingerbread? Once you try it, you're likely to agree that it's the best gingerbread ever! Warm from the oven or at room temperature, this cake is heady with spices and dark with the fragrance of chocolate.

2 eggs
1 cup sugar
½ cup molasses
⅓ cup honey
1½ sticks (¾ cup) butter or margarine, melted
1 cup water
1¼ cups flour
1 cup whole wheat flour
½ cup unsweetened cocoa powder, sifted if lumpy
1 teaspoon baking soda
1 teaspoon cinnamon
1 teaspoon ginger
¼ teaspoon salt

Yield: 18 servings

1. Preheat the oven to 350°F.
2. Grease and flour a 9- x 13-inch baking pan.
3. In a large bowl, beat the eggs. Gradually beat in the sugar, continuing to beat until the mixture is thick and pale. Beat in the molasses and honey, then the melted butter. Stir in the water.
4. In another bowl, stir together the flours, cocoa, baking soda, cinnamon, ginger, and salt. Add to the egg mixture, beating or stirring until the dry ingredients are incorporated.
5. Pour the batter into the prepared pan. Bake the cake for 40 to 45 minutes, or until a toothpick inserted in the center comes out clean. Transfer to a rack to cool.

Boston Cream Pie

*A*s just about everyone knows, Boston Cream Pie isn't a pie at all. Rather, it's a delicious golden layer cake, sandwiched together with rich custard (similar to the filling of an eclair), and covered on top with a dark chocolate glaze. This Boston Cream Pie takes these same elements, but turns them all to chocolate with spectacular results. The custard filling, especially, is particularly delectable—dark, rich, and velvety.

Boston Cream Pie used to be found only at diner-style restaurants, but the dessert is making a well-deserved comeback and is now served in fine American-style restaurants.

CAKE LAYERS

- **2 sticks (1 cup) butter or margarine, softened**
- **2 cups sugar**
- **2 eggs**
- **1 cup buttermilk, or place 1 tablespoon of vinegar in a measuring cup and add milk to come to the 1-cup mark**
- **1 teaspoon vanilla**
- **2 cups minus 2 tablespoons flour**
- **1 teaspoon baking soda**
- **½ cup unsweetened cocoa powder, sifted if lumpy**
- **pinch of salt**

CUSTARD FILLING

- **4 egg yolks**
- **⅔ cup sugar**
- **3 tablespoons flour**
- **1 cup boiling milk**
- **1 tablespoon butter or margarine**
- **½ cup semi-sweet chocolate morsels**

1. First, make the cake layers: Preheat the oven to 375°F.
2. Grease and flour two 9-inch round layer cake pans.
3. In a large bowl, cream the butter with the sugar, continuing to beat until the sugar is fully incorporated. Beat in the eggs, buttermilk, and vanilla.
4. In another bowl, stir together the flour, baking soda, cocoa, and salt. Add to the creamed mixture, beating or stirring until the dry ingredients are incorporated.
5. Divide the batter evenly between the two baking pans. Bake the layers for 30 minutes, or until a toothpick inserted in the center comes out clean. Transfer the pans to a rack to cool. When cool, remove from the pans. Do not fill the layers until completely cooled.
6. Now, make the filling: In a medium-size, heavy saucepan, beat the egg yolks and sugar with a wire whisk until the mixture is thick and pale. Beat in the flour. Gradually add the boiling milk.
7. Place the saucepan over medium heat and cook, stirring constantly, until the mixture comes to a boil and thickens. Let cook for 1 minute longer, stirring constantly.
8. Remove the saucepan from the heat and add the butter and chocolate. Stir until melted.

CHOCOLATE GLAZE
   1 1-ounce square unsweetened chocolate
   1 tablespoon butter or margarine
   2 ½ tablespoons hot water
   ¼ teaspoon vanilla
   ⅔ cup confectioners' sugar

   Yield: 10 to 12 servings

9. Transfer the custard to a bowl and place in the refrigerator until chilled.
10. Place one cake layer, right side up, on a serving plate. Spread the custard filling evenly over the layer. Place the second cake layer, right side up, on top of the filling.
11. Make the chocolate glaze: In a small saucepan, heat the chocolate and butter until melted. Remove from the heat and stir in the hot water and vanilla. Add the confectioners' sugar and beat until the icing is smooth. Immediately spread over the top of the top cake layer.

Note: The cake is best served at room temperature. If you are serving it on the day it is made, you may keep it at room temperature. If serving at a later time, refrigerate the cake and bring to room temperature before serving.

Yam Cake

*L*ike the ever-popular carrot cake, yam cakes are fragrant with spices, wonderfully moist, and have an appealing texture from the grated vegetable. Chocolate Yam Cake is especially dark and richly flavored. This cake keeps fresh for days, so it's an ideal choice for shipping. To turn this into an ultimate dessert, top each slice of cake with a scoop of rum-raisin ice cream.

1 stick (½ cup) butter or margarine
2 cups grated raw yams
2 eggs
1½ cups sugar
¼ cup dark rum
1½ cups flour
⅔ cup unsweetened cocoa powder, sifted if lumpy
1½ teaspoons cinnamon
1 teaspoon baking soda
1 teaspoon baking powder
¼ teaspoon ground cloves
¼ teaspoon nutmeg
⅛ teaspoon salt

Yield: 12 servings

1. Melt the butter in a saucepan. Add the yams and cook, stirring frequently, for 5 minutes. Remove from the heat and let cool slightly.
2. Preheat the oven to 350°F.
3. Grease and flour a 9- x 5-inch loaf pan.
4. In a large bowl, beat the eggs. Gradually beat in the sugar, continuing to beat until the mixture is thick and pale. Beat in the yam mixture, then the rum.
5. In another bowl, stir together the flour, cocoa, cinnamon, baking soda, baking powder, cloves, nutmeg, and salt. Add to the yam mixture, beating or stirring until the dry ingredients are incorporated.
6. Turn the batter into the prepared pan. Bake for 1 hour, 10 minutes, or until a toothpick inserted in the center comes out clean. Transfer the pan to a rack to cool.

Honey Cake

*H*oney cake, a type of spice cake that relies on honey as the primary sweetener, is dense, flavorful, and satisfying. Also, since honey attracts moisture from the air, the cake remains fresh-tasting for longer than most. Chocolate enhances the aroma of the spices in the batter, and a delicate sprinkling of chocolate chips adds to the cake's appeal.

½ stick (4 tablespoons) butter or margarine

3 1-ounce squares unsweetened chocolate

4 eggs

1 cup sugar

1⅓ cups honey

1 tablespoon instant coffee powder, dissolved in 1⅓ cups water

2½ cups flour

1 cup whole wheat flour

2½ teaspoons baking powder

1 teaspoon baking soda

1 teaspoon cinnamon

⅛ teaspoon ginger

⅛ teaspoon ground cloves

⅛ teaspoon salt

½ cup finely ground semi-sweet chocolate (or use mini chocolate chips)

Yield: 18 to 20 servings

1. In a saucepan, heat the butter with the chocolate until melted. Set aside.
2. Preheat the oven to 350°F.
3. Grease and flour a tube pan.
4. In a large bowl, beat the eggs. Gradually beat in the sugar and honey, continuing to beat until the mixture is thick. Beat in the melted chocolate mixture, then the coffee mixture.
5. In another bowl, stir together the flours, baking powder, baking soda, cinnamon, ginger, cloves, and salt. Add to the honey mixture, beating or stirring until the dry ingredients are incorporated. Stir in the semi-sweet chocolate.
6. Turn the batter into the prepared pan. Bake the cake for 1¼ hours, or until a toothpick inserted in the highest part of the cake comes out clean. Transfer the pan to a rack to cool.

Jelly Roll

I remember often having jelly rolls when I was a child, but I rarely encounter them now. This is a pity, as a well-made jelly roll is truly delicious; it is an exceptionally light sponge cake, rolled up with just a thin layer of raspberry jam. I can recall the dessert almost melting in my mouth.

This jelly roll starts with a chocolate sponge cake, and the filling is enhanced with small bits of semi-sweet chocolate. The dessert tastes very much like a raspberry-chocolate bonbon and is so marvelous, it's hard to resist having seconds or even thirds.

4 eggs, separated
1 cup sugar
1 teaspoon vanilla
½ cup flour
**¼ cup unsweetened cocoa powder, sifted
    if lumpy**
¾ teaspoon baking powder
⅛ teaspoon salt
**confectioners' sugar, preferably choco-
    late flavored, for rolling the cake**
½ cup seedless raspberry jam
**¼ cup coarsely chopped semi-sweet
    chocolate**

Yield: 10 to 12 servings

1. In a bowl, beat the egg whites until stiff. Set aside.
2. Preheat the oven to 375°F.
3. Line an 11- x 16-inch shallow baking pan with waxed paper, and grease the paper.
4. In another bowl, beat the egg yolks. Gradually beat in the sugar, continuing to beat until the mixture is thick and pale. Beat in the vanilla.
5. In a small bowl, stir together the flour, cocoa, baking powder, and salt. Add to the bowl with the egg yolks and beat or stir until the dry ingredients are incorporated. The batter will be very stiff. Vigorously stir in about one-third of the beaten egg whites, which will lighten the batter considerably. Fold in the rest of the egg whites gently but thoroughly.
6. Spread the batter evenly in the prepared pan. Bake the cake for about 12 minutes, or until a toothpick inserted in the center comes out clean.
7. While the cake is baking, spread a clean dish towel on the counter, and sprinkle generously with confectioners' sugar. When the cake comes out of the oven, immediately tip it upside down on the dish towel. Beginning with a long side of the rectangle, roll up the cake tightly (including the waxed paper). Place the roll on a rack to cool.

8. When the cake is fully cooled, gently unroll it and peel off the waxed paper. Spread the cake evenly with the jam and sprinkle with the chocolate. Roll the cake up again and transfer it to a serving dish. To make it easier to transfer, cut the cake in half, so you have two, smaller jelly rolls.

Upside Down Cake

*T*raditionally, this is a light, yellow cake that's baked in a skillet that has been coated with a buttery brown sugar mixture and adorned with pineapple rings. Pineapple Upside Down Cake is a delightful combination of carmelized fruit and delicate cake.

Chocolate Upside Down Cake is even better. The pineapple rings are replaced with sweet dark cherries and enhanced with chocolate chips. The batter, while still light and fluffy, has a deep, satisfying chocolate flavor. It makes a wonderful Valentine's Day offering!

TOPPING

- ½ **stick (4 tablespoons) butter or margarine**
- ⅔ **cup brown sugar, preferably dark**
- 1 **16-ounce can dark sweet pitted cherries, drained (reserve ¼ cup liquid for the cake batter)**
- ⅓ **cup semi-sweet chocolate morsels**

BATTER

- 1 **stick (½ cup) butter or margarine, softened**
- 1½ **cups sugar**
- 2 **eggs**
- 1 **cup milk**
- 1 **teaspoon vanilla**
- 2 **cups flour**
- ½ **cup unsweetened cocoa powder, sifted if lumpy**
- 1 **tablespoon baking powder**
- ¼ **teaspoon salt**

Yield: 12 to 14 servings

1. Prepare the topping: In a heavy, ovenproof skillet, melt the butter on top of the stove. Remove the skillet from the heat and stir in the brown sugar, spreading the mixture evenly on the bottom of the skillet. Arrange the cherries in the pan and sprinkle with the chocolate morsels.
2. Preheat the oven to 350°F.
3. Make the cake batter: In a large bowl, cream the butter with the sugar, continuing to beat until the sugar is fully incorporated. Beat in the eggs. Add the milk, the reserved cherry liquid, and vanilla, and beat well.
4. In another bowl, stir together the flour, cocoa, baking powder, and salt. Add to the creamed mixture, beating or stirring until the dry ingredients are incorporated.
5. Carefully spread the batter over the cherries in the skillet. Bake the cake for 50 minutes, or until a toothpick inserted in the center comes out clean.
6. Turn off the oven. Carefully tip the cake out of the skillet onto a heatproof platter. If any of the topping mixture has stuck to the bottom of the skillet, scrape it off with a knife and spread over the top of the cake. Return the cake (on the platter) to the hot oven for 5 minutes, or until the topping is set. Transfer the plate to a rack to cool.

White Chocolate Fudge Cake with White Chocolate Icing

*W*hite chocolate is made from cocoa butter, so it has the texture and velvety smoothness of chocolate without the chocolate flavor. Although chocoholics may miss the chocolate taste, this is a wonderful cake, with the velvety moistness of a true fudge cake. The cake is even richer and more attractive when covered with White Chocolate Icing.

CAKE

- **1 stick (½ cup) butter, softened**
- **1½ cups sugar**
- **2 eggs**
- **3 1-ounce squares white chocolate, melted**
- **1 cup buttermilk, or place 1 tablespoon vinegar in a measuring cup and add enough milk to the 1-cup mark**
- **2 teaspoons vanilla**
- **1⅔ cups flour**
- **1 teaspoon baking powder**
- **½ teaspoon baking soda**
- **⅛ teaspoon salt**

WHITE CHOCOLATE ICING

- **3 1-ounce squares white chocolate**
- **½ stick (4 tablespoons) butter**
- **1 cup plus 2 tablespoons confectioners' sugar**
- **1 egg**
- **1½ tablespoons water**
- **2 teaspoons vanilla**

Yield: 16 servings

1. Preheat the oven to 350°F.
2. Grease and flour a tube pan.
3. Prepare the cake: In a large bowl, cream the butter with the sugar, beating until the sugar is fully incorporated. Beat in the eggs, then the white chocolate, buttermilk, and vanilla.
4. In another bowl, stir together the flour, baking powder, baking soda, and salt. Add to the creamed mixture, beating or stirring until the dry ingredients are incorporated.
5. Spread the batter evenly in the prepared pan. Bake the cake for about 55 minutes, or until a toothpick inserted in the highest part of the cake comes out clean. Transfer the pan to a rack to cool. When cool, remove from the pan. Do not frost until cake has cooled completely.
6. Prepare the icing: In a small saucepan, melt the white chocolate and butter over very low heat.
7. In a large bowl, beat together the confectioners' sugar, egg, water, and vanilla. Place this bowl in a larger bowl or pot filled with ice cubes. Add the melted chocolate mixture. Beat the icing on high speed until thick. The icing will have the texture of whipped cream.
8. Spread the icing over the top and down the sides of the cake.

Note: A cake frosted with this icing needs to be refrigerated if not entirely eaten on the day it is made.

Election Cake

*R*ecipes for Election Cake date back to the American Revolution and contain yeast, rather than baking powder or baking soda, as the rising agent. Election Cake is a raisin-spice cake and not overly sweet. It's somewhat like a date-and-nut loaf, so it is perfect for a between-meal snack. One can only imagine the delight of early American colonists if they had been given a chocolate *Election Cake* with which to celebrate their newly elected officials.

1½ **teaspoons active dry yeast**
⅓ **cup plus ¼ cup brown sugar, prefer-ably dark, divided**
¾ **cup lukewarm milk**
⅓ **cup unsweetened cocoa powder**
½ **teaspoon cinnamon**
¼ **teaspoon nutmeg**
¼ **teaspoon salt**
1¾ **cups flour**
½ **cup raisins**
¾ **stick (6 tablespoons) butter or margarine, softened**
⅓ **cup granulated sugar**
1 **egg**

Yield: 10 to 12 slices

1. In a large bowl, stir together the yeast, ⅓ cup brown sugar, milk, cocoa, cinnamon, nutmeg, and salt. Gradually stir in the flour, and knead until the flour is incorporated. Knead in the raisins.
2. Cover the bowl, and let rise in a warm, draft-free spot for about 1 hour.
3. In another large bowl, cream the butter with the granulated sugar and the remaining ¼ cup brown sugar, continuing to beat until the sugar is fully incorporated. Beat in the egg. Then beat in the risen dough.
4. Grease and flour a 9- x 5-inch loaf pan. Form the dough into a loaf shape and place in the pan. Cover the pan, and let the dough rise for about 45 minutes.
5. Shortly before the dough has finished rising, preheat the oven to 350°F.
6. Bake the cake for 50 minutes, or until a toothpick inserted in the center comes out clean. Transfer the pan to a rack to cool.

New Chocolate Classics

Huguenot Torte

A *true torte contains no flour. However, American bakers, to make a cake sound fancier, often call it a torte. Huguenot Torte is an old southern recipe from Charleston, South Carolina. Except for the one-third cup of flour, it is a torte in that the batter contains finely ground ingredients—in this case, walnuts, pecans, and apples. I've added chocolate, to make an even more delicious dessert.*

½ cup pecans
½ cup walnuts
½ cup semi-sweet chocolate morsels
2 tablespoons sugar plus 1 cup, divided
⅓ cup flour
3 tablespoons unsweetened cocoa powder
3 eggs
1 cup peeled, seeded, and finely chopped apples

Yield: 10 servings

1. Preheat the oven to 350°F.
2. Grease and flour an 8-inch-square baking pan.
3. In the food processor, grind the pecans, walnuts, chocolate, and 2 tablespoons sugar until finely ground. Transfer the mixture to a bowl, and stir in the flour and cocoa.
4. In a large bowl, beat the eggs. Gradually beat in the 1 cup sugar, continuing to beat until the mixture is thick and pale. Stir in the apples, then the nut mixture.
5. Spread the batter evenly in the prepared pan. Bake for 30 to 35 minutes or until a toothpick inserted in the center comes out clean. Transfer to a rack to cool. Serve at room temperature.

Lane Cake

This is a classic southern recipe, as is apparent by its height (southern bakers competed to make the tallest cakes) and ample quantities of pecans, coconut, bourbon, butter, and eggs. In short, Lane Cake is truly wonderful, and this chocolate version—with chocolate cake layers and chocolate truffle filling—makes an exceptional grand finale to any meal.

Note: Although this dessert can be eaten on the day it is made, it is even better the following day, when the cake layers will have absorbed some of the flavors of the filling.

CAKE LAYERS
- **8 egg whites**
- **2 sticks (1 cup) butter or margarine, softened**
- **3 cups sugar**
- **4 1-ounce squares unsweetened chocolate, melted**
- **1 cup milk**
- **3⅔ cups flour**
- **1 tablespoon baking powder**
- **¼ teaspoon salt**

FILLING
- **8 egg yolks**
- **1½ cups sugar**
- **2 1-ounce squares unsweetened chocolate**
- **¼ teaspoon salt**
- **1 stick (½ cup) butter or margarine**
- **1 cup chopped pecans**
- **1 cup raisins**
- **1 cup coconut**
- **1 cup semi-sweet chocolate morsels**
- **½ cup bourbon**

FOR CAKE ASSEMBLY
- **3 tablespoons bourbon**

1. Prepare the cake layers: In a large bowl, beat the egg whites until stiff. Set aside.
2. Preheat the oven to 375°F.
3. Grease and flour two 9-inch-round cake pans.
4. In a large bowl, cream the butter with the sugar, continuing to beat until the sugar is fully incorporated. Beat in the melted chocolate. Add the milk and beat until mixed in.
5. In another bowl, stir together the flour, baking powder, and salt. Add to the chocolate mixture, stirring until the dry ingredients are incorporated. The batter will be very stiff.
6. Vigorously stir in about one-third of the beaten egg whites to lighten the batter. Then fold in the rest of the egg whites gently but thoroughly.
7. Divide the batter evenly between the two prepared pans.
8. Bake the cake for 35 to 40 minutes, or until a toothpick inserted in the center comes out clean. Immediately run a knife around the edge of each pan to loosen the cake from the pan. Then let the layers sit on a rack until cool. When cooled, remove the layers from the pans and split each layer in half horizontally.
9. Prepare the filling: Place the egg yolks, sugar, unsweetened chocolate, salt, and butter in the top of a double

Yield: 25 servings

boiler. Cook over boiling water, stirring frequently, until the butter and chocolate have melted. Then continue to cook, stirring occasionally, for another 30 minutes.

10. Meanwhile, in a large bowl, stir together the pecans, raisins, coconut, and chocolate.

11. When the mixture in the double boiler has finished cooking, remove the pan from the heat and stir in the bourbon, mixing until it is fully incorporated. Pour the mixture into the bowl with the pecans and stir well. Let sit until completely cooled, about 1 hour.

12. Assemble the cake: Place one cake layer, cut side up, on a serving plate. Spread with one-third of the filling mixture. Place another cake layer on top, cut side down, and sprinkle with 1 tablespoon bourbon. Spread with another one-third of the filling. Place a third cake layer, cut side up on top, sprinkle with a tablespoon of bourbon, and spread with the remaining filling. Top with the last cake layer, cut side down, and sprinkle with the remaining tablespoon of bourbon. Cover the cake with plastic wrap until ready to serve.

Lightening Cake

*T*his is an old-fashioned American recipe, developed at a time when most cakes called for separating the eggs and beating the whites until stiff. Usually, when making cakes the butter was only slightly softened, but for this cake it is nearly melted, so it gets beaten into the batter very quickly.

The topping is attractive, chocolaty, and crunchy.

CAKE BATTER
1⅔ **cups flour**
⅓ **cup unsweetened cocoa powder, sifted if lumpy**
¼ **teaspoon salt**
1½ **cups sugar**
2 **eggs**
⅔ **cup milk**
⅔ **cup (10⅔ tablespoons) butter, left on the counter or microwaved until as soft as mayonnaise**
1½ **teaspoons baking powder**

TOPPING
½ **cup confectioners' sugar**
2 **tablespoons unsweetened cocoa powder**
¼ **cup mini semi-sweet chocolate chips**

Yield: 16 servings

1. Preheat the oven to 350°F.
2. Grease a 9- x 9-inch-square baking pan.
3. In a large bowl, stir together the flour, cocoa, salt, and sugar. Add the eggs and milk and beat with an electric mixer until smooth. Add the butter and beat until it is incorporated into the batter. Beat in the baking powder.
4. Spread the batter evenly in the prepared pan. Mix together the ingredients for the topping and sprinkle evenly over the batter.
5. Bake the cake for 45 minutes, or until a toothpick inserted in the center comes out clean. Transfer the pan to a rack to cool.

Hunter Torte

*T*his traditional torte contains finely ground almonds as a replacement for flour. After baking, the torte is covered with a layer of raspberry jam and almond meringue. The result is an Old-World dessert that's elegant and most attractive. Chocolate Hunter Torte uses finely ground semi-sweet chocolate along with nuts, and also includes chocolate meringue, making this a dessert that will please the most diehard of chocoholics.

Note: Because of the meringue topping, the torte cannot be tipped upside down to remove it from the pan. Either serve it directly from the baking pan or use a pan with removable sides.

TORTE

3 egg whites
6 egg yolks
⅔ cup sugar
1 teaspoon vanilla
1 cup finely ground blanched almonds
¾ cup finely ground semi-sweet chocolate

TOPPING

3 egg whites
½ cup sugar
¼ cup unsweetened cocoa powder
¾ cup finely ground blanched almonds
½ cup finely ground semi-sweet chocolate
½ cup seedless raspberry jam

Yield: 12 servings

1. Preheat the oven to 350°F.
2. Grease a tube pan (preferably with removable sides).
3. In a bowl, beat the egg whites until stiff. Set aside.
4. In another bowl, beat the egg yolks. Gradually beat in the sugar, continuing to beat until the mixture is thick and pale. Beat in the vanilla. Then add the ground nuts and chocolate.
5. Stir about one-third of the egg whites into the nut mixture to lighten the batter. Then fold in the rest of the egg whites gently but thoroughly.
6. Turn the batter into the prepared pan. Bake the torte for 25 minutes.
7. While the torte is baking, prepare the topping: With clean bowl and beaters, beat the egg whites until stiff. Gradually beat in the sugar, continuing to beat until the mixture is glossy. Beat in the cocoa. Stir in the almonds and chocolate.
8. When the torte has baked for 25 minutes, remove it from the oven. Quickly spread the raspberry jam in an even layer over the top. Cover with the meringue mixture.
9. Return the torte to the oven and bake for 20 minutes longer. Transfer the pan to a rack to cool. When cool, remove the sides of the pan.

Cakes Never Had It So Good

Dacquoise

*D*acquiose, a flourless layer cake, has a rich buttercream filling sandwiched between crisp meringue layers. Chocolate icing covers the top and drips enticingly down the sides. The dessert offers a wonderful contrast between the sweet, crunchy meringue and the devastatingly rich filling and icing. This Dacquoise, created for chocolate lovers, has ground chocolate flecks in the meringue and an exceedingly deep, dark chocolate buttercream.

MERINGUE LAYERS
- 8 **egg whites**
- ¼ teaspoon **cream of tartar**
- ⅛ teaspoon **salt**
- 1 cup **confectioners' sugar**
- 1 cup **granulated sugar**
- 1 **1-ounce square unsweetened chocolate, finely ground**
- ½ cup **semi-sweet chocolate morsels, finely ground**

BUTTERCREAM
- 6 ounces **semi-sweet chocolate**
- 2 **1-ounce squares unsweetened chocolate**
- 2 **sticks (1 cup) butter, softened**
- 4 **egg whites**
- ½ cup **sugar**

ICING
- ½ cup **heavy or whipping cream**
- 1½ tablespoons **butter**
- 4 ounces **semi-sweet chocolate**

Yield: 16 servings

1. First make the meringue layers: Preheat the oven to 250°F.
2. Using a 9-inch-round cake layer pan as a guide, cut out three circles from waxed paper. Place the paper circles on baking sheets.
3. In a large bowl, beat the egg whites with the cream of tartar and salt until almost stiff. Gradually beat in the confectioners' sugar, then the granulated sugar. Stir in the ground chocolates.
4. Spread the meringue on the paper circles, using one-third of the meringue for each. Use a knife to make even layers.
5. Bake the layers for 1 hour. Reduce the oven temperature to 200°F and bake for 2 hours longer. Transfer the pans to a rack to cool. After about ½ hour, the layers can be removed and the paper peeled off the bottom.
6. In a large saucepan, melt the chocolates for the buttercream. Remove from the heat and stir in the butter. Beat until the butter melts. Chill for just a few minutes, until the mixture is no longer liquidy. Do not chill too long or it will harden.
7. In a large bowl, beat the egg whites until stiff. Gradually beat in the sugar, continuing to beat until the mixture is glossy. Fold the egg whites into the chocolate mixture.
8. Drop about 2 tablespoons of buttercream into the center of a serving plate and place one meringue layer over it.

(The buttercream holds the meringue layer in place, so it won't slide on the plate.) Spread nearly half the remaining buttercream over the meringue layer. Cover with the second meringue layer and most of the rest of the buttercream. Cover with the third meringue layer. Spread the remaining buttercream in a thin layer over the top meringue layer.

9. Chill the cake for at least 45 minutes.

10. Make the icing: In a small saucepan, heat all the ingredients, stirring until smooth. Remove from the heat and cool to room temperature.

11. Spread the icing over the chilled cake, allowing it to drip down the sides. Chill the cake again. The cake should be served cold.

Austrian Walnut Torte

NUSSTORTE

*F*inely ground walnuts, coffee, and dark rum flavor this rich, virtually flourless torte that's sandwiched together with whipped cream. Chocolate Nusstorte is especially luscious, with chocolate cake layers and filling.

TORTE
- **8 eggs, separated**
- **1¼ cups sugar**
- **1½ cups finely ground walnuts**
- **2 tablespoons fine dry bread crumbs**
- **⅓ cup unsweetened cocoa powder**
- **1½ tablespoons strong brewed coffee**
- **1½ tablespoons dark rum**

WHIPPED CREAM
- **2 tablespoons unsweetened cocoa powder**
- **¼ cup sugar**
- **1 cup (½ pint) heavy or whipping cream**

Yield: 10 servings

1. Preheat the oven to 350°F.
2. Butter two 9-inch layer pans, and line the pans with waxed paper. (This cake is fragile and somewhat difficult to remove from the pans, so it is necessary to line them.)
3. In a large bowl, beat the egg whites until stiff. Set aside.
4. In another large bowl, beat the egg yolks. Gradually beat in the sugar, continuing to beat until the mixture is thick and pale. Beat in the walnuts, bread crumbs, cocoa, coffee, and rum.
5. Stir about one-third of the egg whites into the egg yolk mixture to lighten it. Then fold in the rest of the egg whites gently but thoroughly.
6. Divide the batter evenly between the two pans. Bake the layers for about 25 minutes, or until a toothpick inserted in the center comes out clean. Transfer the pans to a rack to cool.
7. While the cake layers are cooling, prepare the whipped cream according to the directions for Chocolate Whipped Cream in the recipe for Strawberry Shortcake (page 50), using the ingredients above. Note that the cocoa and sugar need to be dissolved in the heavy cream at least 1 hour before whipping it.
8. Shortly before serving, place one cake layer, right side up, on a serving plate. Cover with half the whipped cream. Place the other cake layer, right side up, on top. Cover the top with the remaining whipped cream. Chill the cake until ready to serve.

New Chocolate Classics

Mandeltorte

A torte is a cake with no flour or butter. Rather, the batter contains finely ground ingredients—most often nuts—and beaten egg whites to make it rise. Mandel is the German word for almonds. This version is deliciously flavored with finely grated semi-sweet chocolate.

6 eggs, separated
1 cup sugar
½ cup ground almonds
½ cup toasted bread crumbs, made from high-quality white bread
½ cup finely ground semi-sweet chocolate
1 teaspoon vanilla
Chocolate Whipped Cream (from Strawberry Shortcake with Chocolate-Covered Strawberries, page 50), optional

Yield: 8 to 10 servings

1. Preheat the oven to 350°F.
2. Grease a tube pan, preferably one with removable sides.
3. In a large bowl, beat the egg whites until stiff. Set aside.
4. In another large bowl, beat the egg yolks. Gradually beat in the sugar, continuing to beat until the mixture is thick and pale yellow. Stir in the almonds, bread crumbs, chocolate, and vanilla.
5. Stir about half the beaten egg whites into the egg yolk mixture. Then fold in the rest of the whites gently but thoroughly.
6. Spread the batter in the prepared pan. Bake the torte for about 40 minutes, or until a toothpick inserted in the deepest part of the cake comes out clean. Transfer the pan to a rack to cool.

Note: The cake will be quite high when it comes from the oven, but it will fall as it cools. Serve the cake with Chocolate Whipped Cream, if desired.

German Wine Cake

*T*his German fall harvest pound-type cake contains port wine, as well as the elusive flavors of rosemary and pepper. When turned to chocolate, the cake is truly superb, with a wonderful texture. It is moister than most pound cakes and so keeps fresh for several days.

2 sticks (1 cup) butter or margarine, softened
3 cups sugar
6 eggs
4 1-ounce squares unsweetened chocolate, melted
¾ cup ruby port wine
4 cups flour
1 tablespoon baking powder
1 teaspoon rosemary, crushed
½ teaspoon black pepper
¼ teaspoon salt

Yield: 20 servings

1. Preheat the oven to 350°F.
2. Butter and flour a tube pan.
3. In a large bowl, cream the butter with the sugar, continuing to beat until the sugar is fully incorporated. Beat in the eggs very well. Then beat in the chocolate and wine.
4. In another bowl, stir together the flour, baking powder, rosemary, pepper, and salt. Add to the chocolate mixture, beating or stirring until the dry ingredients are incorporated.
5. Turn the batter into the prepared pan. Bake the cake for 1 hour, 20 minutes, or until a toothpick inserted in the highest portion of the cake comes out clean. Transfer the pan to a rack to cool.

French Pound Cake

QUATRE-QUARTS

*Q*uatre-quarts *is the French term for pound cake and translates to "four quarters," mean-ing equal quantities butter, flour, eggs, and sugar. I was confused by this since most pound cake recipes call for about twice as much flour as the other specified ingredients. I then checked* Larousse Gastronomique, *which, oddly enough, offers the same definition for* quatre-quarts, *while at the same time providing a recipe calling for twice as much flour as eggs, butter, and sugar. So much for French precision!*

This chocolate Quatre-quarts is also flavored with coffee and brandy. It's not too sweet and slices beautifully.

1 cup semi-sweet chocolate
⅓ cup brandy
2 teaspoons instant coffee powder
2 sticks (1 cup) butter or margarine, softened
1 cup sugar
6 eggs
2 cups minus 2 tablespoons flour
1 tablespoon baking powder
⅛ teaspoon salt

Yield: 12 to 14 servings

1. In a saucepan, melt the chocolate with the brandy and coffee powder, stirring occasionally. Set aside.
2. Preheat the oven to 325°F.
3. Grease and flour a tube pan.
4. In a large bowl, cream the butter with the sugar, continuing to beat until the sugar is fully incorporated. Beat in the eggs, then the chocolate mixture.
5. In another bowl, stir together the flour, baking powder, and salt. Add to the chocolate mixture, beating or stirring until the dry ingredients are incorporated.
6. Turn the batter into the prepared pan. Bake the cake for 1 hour, 10 minutes, or until a toothpick inserted in the highest part of the cake comes out clean. Transfer the pan to a rack to cool.

Opera Torte

*O*pera Torte is the Austrian version of Boston Cream Pie. Four light layers (called torte, rather than cake, since they contain no flour) are put together with a rich custard and then finished with a marzipan topping. Chocolate Opera Torte is even more spectacular and makes a most elegant ending to an elaborate dinner party.

CAKE LAYERS
- 2 cups confectioners' sugar, divided
- 1⅓ cups cornstarch
- ⅓ cup unsweetened cocoa powder
- 6 eggs, separated
- ¼ teaspoon cream of tartar
- ¼ cup water
- 1 teaspoon vanilla

FILLING
- 1 envelope plain gelatin
- ¼ cup water
- 4 egg yolks
- ½ cup sugar
- 3 tablespoons cornstarch
- 2 1-ounce squares unsweetened chocolate
- 2 cups milk
- 1 teaspoon vanilla
- 1 cup heavy or whipping cream
- 3 tablespoons crème de cacao

TOPPING
- 2 1-ounce squares unsweetened chocolate
- 1 8-ounce can almond paste
  about 2 tablespoons chocolate confectioners' sugar

Yield: about 14 servings

1. Prepare the cake layers: Preheat the oven to 350°F.
2. Grease and flour two 9-inch-round layer pans.
3. In a small bowl, sift together 1 cup confectioners' sugar, cornstarch, and cocoa. Set aside.
4. In a large bowl, beat the egg whites with the cream of tartar until stiff. Gradually beat in the remaining 1 cup confectioners' sugar.
5. In another large bowl, beat the egg yolks well. Beat in the water and vanilla. Beat in the dry ingredients, just until incorporated. Stir about one-third of the egg whites into the batter to lighten it, and then fold in the rest, gently but thoroughly.
6. Divide the batter between the two prepared pans. Bake the layers for about 20 minutes, or until a toothpick inserted in the center comes out clean.
7. Transfer the pans to a rack to cool. When completely cool, remove the cake from the pans. Cut each layer in half horizontally to make 4 cake layers.
8. Prepare the filling: Dissolve the gelatin in the water. Let sit for 5 minutes to soften.
9. In the top of a double boiler, over boiling water, place the egg yolks, sugar, cornstarch, chocolate, and milk. Cook, stirring constantly, until the mixture is thick and smooth. Remove the top of the double boiler from the heat, and stir in the vanilla and gelatin mixture.

10. Transfer the mixture to a bowl and chill, stirring occasionally, until nearly set.

11. In a large bowl, beat the heavy cream until stiff. Beat in the crème de cacao. Fold the cream mixture into the rest of the filling mixture. Chill until firm.

12. On a serving plate, place one cake layer, cut side up. Spread one-quarter of the filling over the cake. Cover with another layer, cut side down. Repeat until all the cake has been used. The top of the cake will be covered with the final one-quarter of the filling. Chill the cake while preparing the topping.

13. Prepare the topping: Melt the chocolate in a small saucepan. Place the almond paste in the food processor. Add the melted chocolate and process until the mixture is smooth.

14. Using the layer cake pan as a guide, draw a 9-inch circle on a piece of waxed paper. Gather the almond mixture into a ball and place on the waxed paper. Using your hands, press the almond mixture into an even layer that fills the circle. Tip upside down on top of the cake and peel off the waxed paper.

15. Place a lacy doily over the top of the cake. Sift the chocolate confectioners' sugar over the doily. Lift the doily gently, so the lacy pattern shows when it is removed. Chill the cake until ready to serve.

Scandinavian Almond-Caramel Cake

TOSKAKAKE

*E*ven in its non-chocolate form, this is a sensational cake. After baking, a creamy mixture is poured over a simple butter cake, and then sprinkled with almonds. It goes back into the oven and emerges with a caramel topping that permeates the inside of the cake as well. Chocolate Toskakake begins with a rich chocolate butter cake, and the top contains semi-sweet chocolate along with the almonds. On tasting it, my daughter promptly declared this the best chocolate cake in the cookbook.

CAKE
3 eggs
1½ cups sugar
⅔ cup (10⅔ tablespoons) butter, melted
3 tablespoons milk
1 teaspoon vanilla
1¼ cups flour
½ cup unsweetened cocoa powder, sifted if lumpy
1½ teaspoons baking powder

TOPPING
⅓ cup (5⅓ tablespoons) butter
½ cup sugar
½ cup heavy or whipping cream
⅓ cup chopped almonds
⅓ cup chopped semi-sweet chocolate

Yield: 12 servings

1. Grease a tube pan with a removable rim.
2. Preheat the oven to 350°F.
3. In a large bowl, beat the eggs. Gradually beat in the sugar, continuing to beat until the mixture is thick and pale. Beat in the melted butter until fully incorporated. Then beat in the milk and vanilla.
4. In another bowl, stir together the flour, cocoa, and baking powder. Add to the egg mixture, beating or stirring until the dry ingredients are fully incorporated.
5. Pour the batter into the prepared pan. Bake for about 40 minutes. The cake will be set and nearly done, but a toothpick inserted into the highest part of the cake will not come out completely clean.
6. While the cake is baking, prepare the topping: In a medium saucepan, melt the butter. Add the sugar and cream. Bring to a boil, stirring to dissolve the sugar. Then boil for 2 minutes, watching carefully to make certain it doesn't boil over the top of the pot. Remove from the heat.
7. After the cake has baked for 40 minutes, pour the topping over it. The topping will look like a big puddle on top of the cake. Sprinkle the topping with the almonds and chocolate.
8. Return the cake to the oven and bake for about 10 minutes longer, or until the topping is mostly absorbed and is bubbly and browned. Transfer the cake to a rack to cool.

Turkish Yogurt Cake

This cake is liberally moistened with syrup as soon as it comes from the oven. Although many Middle Eastern desserts of this sort are cloyingly sweet, the addition of bitter chocolate and unsweetened cocoa makes this no more sugary than any American dessert— and just as delicious! Furthermore, the cake contains no butter or oil, so it is quite low in fat.

Note: Because this cake is so moist, leftovers should be stored in the refrigerator. Bring to room temperature before serving.

CHOCOLATE SYRUP
1½ cups water
1¼ cups sugar
2 1-ounce squares unsweetened
   chocolate

CAKE
3 eggs
1 cup sugar
1 cup plain yogurt
1 teaspoon grated orange rind
1 cup flour
½ cup unsweetened cocoa powder,
   sifted if lumpy
1 teaspoon baking powder

Yield: about 26 pastries

1. First make the syrup: Place the water, sugar, and chocolate in a saucepan. Cook, stirring frequently, until the sugar is dissolved and the chocolate melts. Continue cooking over a medium heat, stirring occasionally, until the mixture forms a light syrup, about 15 minutes. Set aside.

2. Meanwhile, make the cake: Preheat the oven to 375°F.

3. Grease and flour a 9-inch-square pan.

4. In a large bowl, beat the eggs. Gradually beat in the sugar, continuing to beat until the mixture is thick and pale. Beat in the yogurt and orange rind.

5. In another bowl, stir together the flour, cocoa, and baking powder. Add to the yogurt mixture, beating or stirring until the dry ingredients are incorporated.

6. Spread the batter evenly in the pan. Bake for 20 to 25 minutes, or until a toothpick inserted in the center of the cake comes out clean.

7. Using a sharp serrated knife, immediately cut the cake into diamond shapes, about 1-inch square. (Do not remove from pan.) Transfer the pan to a rack, and pour the chocolate syrup over the cake. Let sit until the syrup is completely absorbed.

Yule Log

Yule Log is a classic Christmas dessert, in which a delicate sponge cake is filled and decorated to look like the branch of a tree. Although a Yule Log is almost always covered with chocolate frosting, the cake and filling are customarily vanilla flavored. This version, which contains chocolate cake, chocolate whipped cream, and a rich chocolate icing, provides three entirely different textures for the luscious chocolate flavor.

CAKE

- 5 **eggs, separated**
- ¼ **teaspoon cream of tartar**
- ½ **cup sugar plus 1 cup, divided**
- 2 **tablespoons brandy**
- ¼ **cup unsweetened cocoa powder, sifted if lumpy**
- ¼ **teaspoon salt**
- ⅞ **cup flour**
- **chocolate confectioners' sugar, for rolling the cake**

FILLING

- 2 **cups (1 pint) heavy or whipping cream**
- ½ **cup sugar**
- ⅓ **cup cocoa powder**

FROSTING

- 3 **1-ounce squares unsweetened chocolate**
- 3 **tablespoons butter or margarine**
- 4 **cups confectioners' sugar**
- ⅛ **teaspoon salt**
- 1 **teaspoon vanilla**
- **approximately 7 tablespoons milk**
- **about ¼ cup finely chopped pistachio nuts**

1. First, make the cake: Preheat the oven to 350°F.
2. Line a 15- x 10-inch baking sheet with foil and butter the foil.
3. In a large bowl, beat the egg whites and cream of tartar until stiff. Gradually beat in ½ cup sugar, continuing to beat until the mixture is thick and glossy. Set aside.
4. In another bowl, beat the egg yolks. Gradually add the remaining 1 cup sugar, continuing to beat until the mixture is thick and pale. Beat in the brandy, cocoa, and salt, then the flour, mixing just until incorporated.
5. Stir about a third of the beaten egg white mixture into the yolk mixture to lighten it, and then fold in the rest of the whites gently but thoroughly.
6. Spread the batter evenly in the prepared pan. Bake for about 20 minutes, or until a toothpick inserted in the center comes out clean.
7. While the cake is baking, spread a clean dish towel on the counter and sprinkle liberally with chocolate confectioners' sugar. As soon as the cake comes from the oven, tip it upside down onto the towel. Remove the foil, and roll up the cake (including the towel), jelly-roll style, beginning with one of the long edges. Let the cake sit rolled up until completely cooled. Do not unroll until ready to fill.

8. Make the filling, following the recipe for Chocolate Whipped Cream from the recipe for Strawberry Shortcake (page 50), using the ingredients listed above.

9. Unroll the cake gently. (It will crack, but don't worry, as the cracks will be covered by the frosting.) Spread the whipped cream evenly over the cake, and roll up again (this time without the dish towel). Transfer the roll to a serving plate. If you wish, you may cut off one or two pieces from the end of the log and put them next to a portion of the center of the log. When frosted, the "log" will appear to have stumps of other branches coming off it.

10. Make the frosting: In a large saucepan, melt the chocolate with the butter. Add the confectioners' sugar, salt, vanilla, and about 5 tablespoons milk. Beat until thick and glossy, adding additional milk until of good spreading consistency.

11. Frost the log. Then, use the tines of a fork to make lines resembling bark and knots. Sprinkle with pistachio nuts. Chill until ready to serve.

Tyrolean Christmas Fruitcake

ZELTEN

*T*he only resemblance between this and American fruitcakes is that they are both packed with fruit, with very little actual cake batter. However, Zelten contains dried fruits rather than candied fruits, as well as pine nuts and almonds. These are macerated for a week in brandy, which lends a wonderful aroma. Additionally, Zelten is made with a yeasted dough, which conveniently requires no kneading.

Chocolate Zelten is dark, fruity, and extremely satisfying on a cold winter day, accompanied by after-dinner brandy. The chocolate glaze enhances its flavor and adds to the cake's attractiveness.

Note: You must begin preparing this cake a week in advance in order for the fruits to absorb the brandy.

CAKE
1½ cups raisins
¼ cup pine nuts
½ cup chopped dried apricots
½ cup finely ground almonds
⅓ cup brandy
⅓ cup unsweetened cocoa powder
½ teaspoon cinnamon
¼ teaspoon ground cloves
1 cup flour
⅔ cup lukewarm milk
2 teaspoons active dry yeast
½ cup sugar

GLAZE
¼ cup strong black coffee
3 tablespoons honey
3 tablespoons unsweetened cocoa powder
2 tablespoons sugar

Yield: 10 servings

1. In a large bowl, stir together the raisins, pine nuts, apricots, almonds, brandy, cocoa, cinnamon, and cloves. Cover the bowl and let sit in a cool spot for about 1 week.
2. On the day you wish to prepare the Zelten, stir together the flour, milk, yeast, and sugar in a large bowl. Cover with plastic wrap and let sit in a warm place for 1 hour.
3. Grease and flour a 9-inch-round layer cake pan.
4. Stir the raisin mixture into the flour mixture. Turn into the prepared pan. Smooth the top to make even. Cover the pan and let sit in a warm place for 1 hour.
5. Preheat the oven to 350°F.
6. Bake the cake for 30 minutes, or until a toothpick inserted in the center comes out clean.
7. While the cake is baking, combine all the ingredients for the glaze in a small saucepan. Cook, stirring, until the mixture comes to a boil. Remove from the heat.
8. When the cake has finished baking, pour the glaze over the top. Transfer the pan to a rack to cool. When cool, cut the cake into wedges.

THE COOKIE
CRUMBLES
TO CHOCOLATE

German Christmas Bars

LEBKUCHEN

*T*his traditional Christmas offering contains honey, ground nuts, and spices and is made even more delicious when flavored with chocolate. The topping of fudge sauce, walnuts, and semi-sweet chocolate makes the bars even more special. Because honey helps retain moisture, these bars keep well so they can be prepared a week or two before the holidays.

Note: The batter needs to rest for 24 hours in the refrigerator before baking the bars.

BARS
- **2 eggs**
- **1 cup honey**
- **¾ cup brown sugar, preferably dark**
- **½ cup brewed tea, cooled**
- **2 tablespoons brandy**
- **2½ cups flour**
- **⅔ cup unsweetened cocoa powder, sifted if lumpy**
- **1 cup ground walnuts**
- **1 cup ground almonds**
- **1 teaspoon baking soda**
- **1 teaspoon baking powder**
- **1 teaspoon cinnamon**
- **½ teaspoon nutmeg**
- **¼ teaspoon salt**
- **⅔ cup semi-sweet chocolate morsels**

TOPPING
- **½ cup fudge ice cream topping**
- **½ cup finely chopped walnuts**
- **½ cup finely chopped semi-sweet chocolate**

Yield: 40 to 50 bars

1. In a large bowl, beat the eggs. Add the honey and brown sugar and continue beating until the mixture is thick. Beat in the tea and brandy.
2. In another bowl, stir together the flour, cocoa, walnuts, almonds, baking soda, baking powder, cinnamon, nutmeg, and salt. Add to the honey mixture, beating or stirring until the dry ingredients are incorporated. Stir in the chocolate morsels.
3. Cover the bowl with plastic and let sit overnight in the refrigerator. Remove from the refrigerator 1 hour before baking the bars.
4. Preheat the oven to 375°F.
5. Grease an 11- x 16-inch baking pan.
6. Spread the dough evenly in the prepared pan. Since the dough will be very sticky, the easiest way to do this is to coat your hands with flour and pat the dough into an even layer.
7. Bake the bars for 18 to 20 minutes, or until a toothpick inserted in the center of the pan comes out nearly clean. Transfer the pan to a rack and let cool completely before covering with the topping.
8. Spread the fudge sauce evenly over the bars. Sprinkle with the walnuts and chocolate, and press down lightly. Cut into bars.

Swedish Spice Cookies

SPECULAAS

These crisp cookies are rolled out and cut into holiday shapes for Christmas. The chocolate complements the delicate spices, making these a most special treat.

1 **stick (½ cup) butter or margarine, softened**
1 **cup brown sugar, preferably dark brown**
1 **egg**
2 **1-ounce squares unsweetened chocolate, melted**
1 **cup flour**
1 **cup whole wheat flour**
1½ **teaspoons baking powder**
1½ **teaspoons cinnamon**
¾ **teaspoon ginger**
¼ **teaspoon nutmeg**
¼ **teaspoon anise seeds**
⅛ **teaspoon salt**
miniature red and green M&M's, for decorating the cookies, if desired

Yield: about 32 2½-inch cookies

1. In a large bowl, cream the butter with the brown sugar, continuing to beat until the sugar is fully incorporated. Beat in the egg, then the melted chocolate.
2. In another bowl, stir together the flours, baking powder, cinnamon, ginger, nutmeg, anise, and salt. Add to the creamed mixture, beating or stirring until the dry ingredients are incorporated.
3. Place the bowl in the refrigerator and chill for at least 2 hours.
4. Preheat the oven to 350°F.
5. Grease two baking sheets.
6. On a lightly floured surface, roll out the cookie dough to ¼ inch thick. Cut into shapes (star, bell, candy cane) with cookie cutters and place, at least an inch apart, on the baking sheets. Decorate the cookies with miniature red and green M&M's, if desired.
7. Place the baking sheets in the oven and bake for about 12 minutes, or until the cookies are firm and lightly browned on the bottoms. Transfer the cookies to a rack to cool.

Almond Wreaths

To make these cookies, you need a cookie press in order to form the dough into attractive wreath shapes. The cookies are dark chocolate, with delicate almond flavoring. They can be decorated with red and green candied cherries for Christmas.

COOKIE DOUGH
- **1 stick (½ cup) butter or margarine, softened**
- **⅔ cup sugar**
- **1 egg**
- **1 teaspoon vanilla**
- **¼ teaspoon almond extract**
- **1 cup flour**
- **½ cup unsweetened cocoa powder, sifted if lumpy**
- **¼ teaspoon baking powder**
- **⅛ teaspoon salt**
- **¼ cup finely ground almonds**

DECORATION
- **1 cup confectioners' sugar**
- **2 tablespoons plus 1 teaspoon milk**
- **candied red and green cherries, optional**

Yield: about 30 2-inch cookies

1. Preheat the oven to 350°F.
2. Grease two baking sheets.
3. In a large bowl, cream the butter with the sugar, continuing to beat until the sugar is fully incorporated. Beat in the egg, then the vanilla and almond extract.
4. In another bowl, stir together the flour, cocoa, baking powder, and salt. Add to the creamed mixture, beating or stirring until the dry ingredients are incorporated. Stir in the almonds.
5. Place the dough in a cookie press, fitted with the star tip. Push the dough out of the bag, forming 2-inch wreath shapes, each about a half-inch apart on the baking sheet.
6. Bake the cookies for 8 to 10 minutes, or until they are firm and the bottoms are lightly browned. Transfer the cookies to a rack to cool.
7. When the cookies have cooled, stir together the confectioners' sugar and milk. Spread this glaze lightly over the top of each cookie. While the glaze is still wet, decorate each wreath with half a candied red cherry. On each side of the cherry, place a quarter of a candied green cherry.

Sugar Cookies

*O*f all cookies, the simple sugar cookie is everyone's favorite. These are just like tradi-tional sugar cookies, except they are chocolate. If making the cookies for Christmas, sprinkle them with red and green crystallized sugar.

1½ sticks (¾ cup) butter or margarine, softened
1½ cups sugar
1 egg
3 1-ounce squares unsweetened chocolate, melted
1 teaspoon vanilla
2½ cups flour
1 teaspoon baking powder
⅛ teaspoon salt
crystallized sugar (plain or red and green)

Yield: about 32 2-inch cookies

1. Preheat the oven to 350°F.
2. Grease two baking sheets.
3. In a large bowl, cream the butter with the sugar, continu-ing to beat until the sugar is fully incorporated. Beat in the egg, then the chocolate and vanilla.
4. In another bowl, stir together the flour, baking powder, and salt. Add to the creamed mixture, beating or stirring until the dry ingredients are incorporated.
5. With lightly floured hands, form the dough into balls, each about 1¼ inches in diameter. Place the balls on the bak-ing sheet. Using the bottom of a drinking glass, flatten each ball into a circle, about ½ inch thick. Sprinkle with the crystallized sugar.
6. Bake the cookies for about 10 minutes, or until firm and lightly browned on the bottoms. Transfer to a rack to cool.

Star Cookies

A rich cream cheese dough makes these cookies positively devastating! Use red and green crystallized sugar if making these for the holidays.

1½ sticks (¾ cup) butter or margarine, softened
1 8-ounce package cream cheese, softened
1½ cups sugar
2 egg yolks
4 1-ounce squares unsweetened chocolate, melted
1 teaspoon vanilla
3 cups flour
1 teaspoon baking powder
crystallized sugar (plain or red and green)

Yield: about 80 2-inch cookies

1. In a large bowl, cream the butter and cream cheese with the sugar, continuing to beat until the sugar is fully incorporated. Beat in the egg yolks, then the chocolate and vanilla.
2. In another bowl, stir together the flour and baking powder. Add to the creamed mixture, beating or stirring until the dry ingredients are incorporated.
3. Place the bowl in the refrigerator and chill until the dough is firm, about 1 hour.
4. Preheat the oven to 325°F.
5. Grease two baking sheets.
6. Working with about one-quarter of the dough at a time, roll out the dough on a lightly floured surface to ¼ inch thick. (Keep the remaining dough in the refrigerator.) Cut with a star-shaped cookie cutter and place the cookies, about ½ inch apart, on the baking sheets. Sprinkle with the crystallized sugar.
7. Bake the cookies for 10 to 12 minutes, or until they are firm and the bottoms are lightly browned. Transfer the cookies to a rack to cool. Continue forming and baking the cookies until all the dough has been used.

New Chocolate Classics

Austrian Almond Butter Cookies

ISCHELER TORTELETTEN

These traditional cookies are sandwiched together with apricot jam and covered with chocolate icing. Even when not chocolate flavored, these cookies make a sensational teatime treat or after-dinner offering. When the Torteletten are made with a chocolate dough, the result is out of this world!

COOKIES
- 2 cups minus 2 tablespoons flour
- 1 cup finely ground blanched almonds
- ½ cup unsweetened cocoa powder, sifted if lumpy
- 1½ cups sugar
- grated rind from ½ lemon
- ½ teaspoon baking powder
- ¼ teaspoon salt
- 2 sticks (1 cup) butter
- 3 to 4 tablespoons water

FILLING AND ICING
- ½ cup apricot jam
- 6 ounces semi-sweet chocolate
- 1 tablespoon butter
- approximately 28 whole blanched almonds

Yield: about 28 sandwich cookies

1. In a large bowl, stir together the flour, almonds, cocoa, sugar, lemon rind, baking powder, and salt. With your fingertips, two knives, or a pastry cutter, cut in the butter until the mixture is the texture of coarse meal. Gradually add the water, using only enough for the dough to form a ball.
2. Wrap the dough in plastic and let chill for at least 2 hours.
3. Preheat the oven to 350°F.
4. Line two baking sheets with waxed paper or grease the sheets well.
5. Work with only about one-quarter of the dough at a time, keeping the rest chilled until ready to use. Roll out the dough to about ¼ inch thick on a lightly floured surface, flouring the rolling pin as well. Cut the dough into rounds with a 2-inch cutter. Place on the prepared baking sheets.
6. Bake the cookies for 10 minutes. (You will need to bake the cookies in batches.) The cookies will still be quite soft, but it is important to remove them from the baking sheets immediately after they come from the oven, or they will stick to the sheets. If you lift the cookies carefully with a spatula, they will not break. The cookies will firm up as they cool.
7. When thoroughly cooled, sandwich pairs of cookies together with a little apricot jam.
8. Melt the chocolate and butter in a small saucepan. Frost the tops of each cookie sandwich with the chocolate mixture, and place a whole almond in the center of each.

Norwegian Ring Cookies

*S*candinavian butter cookies are undeniably rich. And these, from Norway, are probably the richest of all, since they contain three egg yolks in addition to plenty of butter. Traditional Ring Cookies are flavored with vanilla; this chocolate version is exceptionally delicious!

DOUGH
  **yolks from 2 hard-boiled eggs,
    mashed**
  1 raw egg yolk
  1¼ cups confectioners' sugar
  1½ sticks (¾ cup) butter, softened
  ½ teaspoon vanilla
  3 tablespoons water
  ⅓ cup unsweetened cocoa powder
  2 cups flour

TOPPING
  1 egg, beaten
  crystallized sugar

Yield: about 2 dozen ring cookies

1. In a large bowl, beat the cooked egg yolks, raw egg yolk, and confectioners' sugar until well mixed. Beat in the butter very well. Beat in the vanilla, water, and cocoa. Stir in the flour, mixing just until incorporated. Chill the dough for at least 1 hour.
2. Preheat the oven to 350°F.
3. Grease two cookie sheets.
4. Form the dough into balls, about 1¼ inches across. Roll the balls between the palms of your hand to make ropes, about 4 inches long. Place each rope on the cookie sheet, and join the ends to form rings.
5. Brush the rings with the beaten egg, and sprinkle with the crystallized sugar.
6. Bake the cookies for 10 to 12 minutes, or until they are firm. Carefully transfer the cookies to a rack or waxed paper to cool.

Austrian Nut Crescents

NUSSKIPFERLN

*T*hese wonderful morsels are similar to shortbread cookies, only crisper and more flavorful from the addition of nuts. The coating of confectioners' sugar makes them particularly attractive.

1½ sticks (¾ cup) butter, softened
1½ cups sugar
  3 1-ounce squares unsweetened
    chocolate, melted
1½ teaspoons vanilla
2½ cups flour
  1 cup finely ground walnuts
  about 1 cup chocolate-flavored
    confectioners' sugar or more if
    needed, for coating the baked
    cookies

Yield: about 40 cookies

1. Preheat the oven to 350°F.
2. Grease two large baking sheets.
3. In a large bowl, cream the butter with the sugar, continuing to beat until the sugar is fully incorporated. Beat in the chocolate, then the vanilla.
4. In another bowl, stir together the flour and walnuts. Add to the creamed mixture, beating or stirring until the dry ingredients are incorporated. The dough will be somewhat crumbly.
5. Gather up about 2 tablespoons of dough and press together so it is no longer crumbly. Form this into a crescent shape, about 2 inches long and ½ inch high. Place on the prepared baking sheet. Continue forming cookies in this manner until all the dough has been used. These cookies do not spread while baking, so you can place them close together on the baking sheet.
6. Bake the cookies for 20 minutes.
7. Spread the chocolate confectioners' sugar on a plate. One by one, transfer the hot cookies to the plate of sugar and roll in the sugar. (It's best to use a fork to handle the cookies, as they are very hot.) Place the cookies on a rack and let cool. Add more confectioners' sugar to the plate as needed. When cool, roll once again in the confectioners' sugar.

Swedish Rye Cookies

*T*hese Swedish cookies are rather soft and moist—somewhat like oatmeal cookies—due to the addition of rye flour. Most Americans have sampled rye flavor only in sour-dough-type rye breads. Rye flour by itself has none of that "sour" taste and just imparts a pleasing wholesomeness to the cookies.

1½ **sticks (¾ cup) butter or margarine, softened**
1½ **cups sugar**
 2 **eggs**
½ **cup unsweetened cocoa powder**
⅛ **teaspoon salt**
⅔ **cup rye flour**
 1 **cup white flour**

Yield: about 60 cookies

1. In a large bowl, cream the butter with the sugar, beating until the sugar is fully incorporated. Beat in the eggs, then the cocoa and salt. Add the rye flour, then the white flour, mixing just until the dry ingredients are incorporated. Place the bowl in the refrigerator and chill for 1 to 2 hours.
2. Preheat the oven to 325°F.
3. Grease two large cookie sheets.
4. On a lightly floured surface, roll out half the dough to between ⅛ and ¼ inch thick. (Keep the remaining dough chilled until ready to use.) Cut the dough into rounds about 2 inches in diameter and place on the cookie sheet. (Since these cookies contain no baking powder, they spread very little and can be placed on the sheet almost touching one another.) Prick each cookie several times with the tines of a fork.
5. Bake the cookies for about 10 minutes, or until baked through. Transfer to a rack to cool.

Scandinavian Shortbread Cookies

UPPÅKRA BISCUITS

*T*hese are positively the best shortbread cookies ever! Rich and chocolaty, they have a unique flavor from the addition of potato starch and a wonderful crunch from the almond-sugar topping.

Note: Potato starch, which is similar in texture to cornstarch, is available in the Jewish foods supermarket aisle.

DOUGH

1½ **sticks (12 tablespoons) butter, softened**

¾ **cup sugar**

2 **1-ounce squares unsweetened chocolate, melted**

3 **tablespoons water**

2 **cups flour**

⅓ **cup potato starch**

TOPPING

2 **eggs, beaten**

sugar cubes (enough to make ⅓ cup when crushed)

½ **cup finely chopped blanched almonds**

Yield: about 34 cookies

1. In a large bowl, cream the butter with the sugar, continuing to beat until the sugar is fully incorporated. Beat in the chocolate and water, then the flour and potato starch.
2. Chill the dough for 1 hour.
3. Preheat the oven to 350°F.
4. Grease two large cookie sheets.
5. Place the beaten eggs in a small bowl. Stir together the crushed sugar and almonds in another bowl.
6. On a lightly floured surface, roll out the dough to just under ¼ inch thick. Cut into rounds with a 2-inch cookie cutter. Fold each round over to make a turnover shape. Dip the top of the cookie into the egg, then dip into the almond-sugar mixture, coating the cookie generously. Place the cookie, sugar side up, on the prepared cookie sheet. (These cookies do not spread while baking, so you can place them quite close together on the sheet.)
7. Bake the cookies for 15 to 18 minutes, or until baked through. Carefully transfer to a rack to cool.

Wine Cookies

*T*hese crispy Italian cookies contain Marsala (similar in taste to sweet sherry). When chocolate is added, the marriage of flavors is superb!

DOUGH
- **2 sticks (1 cup) butter or margarine, softened (try to use at least half butter if possible)**
- **2 cups sugar**
- **2 egg yolks**
- **²⁄₃ cup sweet Marsala**
- **4½ cups flour**
- **⅛ teaspoon salt**
- **²⁄₃ cup unsweetened cocoa powder, sifted if lumpy**

TOPPING
- **2 egg whites, beaten slightly with a fork**
- **½ cup finely chopped walnuts**
- **½ cup finely chopped semi-sweet chocolate**

Yield: 60 cookies

1. In a large bowl, cream the butter with the sugar until the sugar is completely incorporated. Beat in the egg yolks, then the Marsala.
2. In another bowl, stir together the flour, salt, and cocoa. Add to the butter mixture, beating or stirring until the dry ingredients are fully incorporated. You may need to use your hands for the mixing as the dough is very stiff.
3. Chill the dough for at least 1 hour.
4. Preheat the oven to 350°F.
5. Grease two baking sheets.
6. Working with about half the dough at a time (and keeping the remaining dough chilled), roll out on a lightly floured surface to slightly more than ¼ inch thick. Cut into rounds with a 2-inch cookie cutter and place on the prepared baking sheet. (The cookies will not spread while baking, so they can be placed close together on the sheet.)
7. Brush the tops of each cookie with the beaten egg whites. Stir together the walnuts and chocolate, and sprinkle on top.
8. Bake the cookies for about 15 minutes, or until firm. Transfer the cookies to a rack to cool.

New Chocolate Classics

Linzer Tarts

Virtually every bakery, deli, and coffeeshop sells Linzer Tarts—large, buttery cookies that are sandwiched together with raspberry jam. The top cookie is ring shaped, so the jam peeks out appealingly from the center. These homemade Linzer Tarts are chocolate flavored, which wonderfully complements the raspberry filling.

COOKIES
- **1 stick (½ cup) butter, softened**
- **¾ cup sugar**
- **2 eggs**
- **2 1-ounce squares unsweetened chocolate, melted**
- **2¼ cups flour**
- **⅓ cup ground walnuts**

FILLING AND TOPPING
- **about ¼ cup seedless raspberry jam**
- **about ½ cup chocolate confectioners' sugar**

Yield: 16 to 18 tarts

Note: Traditionally, Linzer Tarts are cut with a scalloped cookie cutter, but if you don't have one, a round cutter (or even a drinking glass) will do fine. The top cookies are ring shaped, so you may use a scalloped ring cutter, or use the same cutter you used for the bottom cookies and cut a 1-inch hole from the center of each. A melon-ball cutter works well for this.

1. In a large bowl, cream the butter with the sugar, continuing to beat until the sugar is fully incorporated. Beat in the eggs, then the chocolate.
2. In another bowl, stir together the flour and walnuts. Add to the chocolate mixture, beating or stirring until the dry ingredients are incorporated.
3. Cover the bowl and chill the dough for 1 to 2 hours.
4. Preheat the oven to 375°F.
5. Grease two cookie sheets.
6. On a lightly floured surface, roll out the dough to ¼ inch thick. Cut equal numbers of 2½-inch rounds and 2½-inch rings, and place on the prepared baking sheets. (The cookies will not spread while baking, so they can be placed close together on the sheets.)
7. Bake the cookies for about 10 minutes, or until firm. Transfer to a rack to cool.
8. When cool, spread each round cookie with a layer of raspberry jam. Sift the chocolate confectioners' sugar over the ring-shaped cookies, and place them on top of the jam-coated bottoms.

The Cookie Crumbles to Chocolate

Amaretti

*A*maretti are crisp, delicate Italian cookies made with no flour, butter, or egg yolks. Their flavor comes from ground almonds and their light texture from egg whites. They make a perfect accompaniment to a variety of desserts, from ice cream and sorbets to after-dinner coffee to fresh fruits.

In this country, Amaretti are usually sold in tins, with the cookies wrapped in pairs. Such Amaretti are delicious, but are somewhat stale tasting compared to the homemade version, which, fortunately, is very easy to make. These chocolate Amaretti are simply wonderful, with dark chocolate contrasting with the ground almonds.

**1 cup plus 2 tablespoons almonds,
    ground to a fine powder**
2¼ cups sugar
**¾ cup unsweetened cocoa powder,
    sifted if lumpy**
½ cup egg whites (about 3 to 4)
¾ teaspoon almond extract

Yield: 40 Amaretti

1. Preheat the oven to 350°F.
2. Line two baking sheets with parchment paper.
3. In a bowl, stir together the ground almonds, sugar, and cocoa.
4. In a large bowl, beat the egg whites with the almond extract, just until frothy. Stir in the almond mixture, mixing until fully incorporated.
5. Drop the dough by teaspoonfuls onto the prepared baking sheets. Each round of dough should be about 1 inch in diameter.
6. Bake the Amaretti for about 20 minutes. The cookies will be firm and slightly shiny with small cracks in the top.
7. Transfer the baking sheets to a rack and let the Amaretti cool to room temperature. With a metal spatula, carefully remove the Amaretti from the paper.

Florentine "Ugly but Good" Cookies

*T*he Italian name for these hearty cookies is Brutti ma Buoni, which translates to "ugly but good." The cookies are wonderfully dense, with a delicious almond flavor that comes from using ground nuts as a substitute for flour. In texture, these are like a cross between amaretti and fruit jumbles—in chocolate, naturally!

Note: This cookie dough is a snap to prepare in the food processor. The almonds can also be ground in a nut grinder, and the dough prepared in a bowl using an electric mixer.

8 ounces blanched almonds (about 1¾ cups)
1½ cups confectioners' sugar
½ cup unsweetened cocoa powder
¼ teaspoon vanilla
¼ teaspoon almond extract
2 eggs
⅓ cup chopped walnuts
3 tablespoons finely minced dried apricots
½ cup mini chocolate chips

Yield: 24 large cookies

1. Preheat the oven to 350°F.
2. Grease a large baking sheet.
3. Place the nuts in the bowl of the food processor and process until finely ground. Add the confectioners' sugar, cocoa, vanilla, and almond extract, and process until well mixed. With the food processor going, add the eggs through the feed tube and process until the mixture forms a ball. Stir in the walnuts, apricots, and chocolate chips.
4. Drop balls of dough, about 1½ to 2 inches in diameter, onto the prepared cookie sheet. Do not make an effort to smooth out any irregular shapes the balls may have. This dough does not spread when the cookies are baked, so you do not need to leave much room between the balls of dough on the cookie sheet.
5. Bake the cookies for about 20 minutes, or until firm. Carefully remove to a rack to cool.

Madelines

Madelines were made famous by Marcel Proust, who so elegantly recorded his recollections of dipping these little cakes into tea, that his words are still read centuries after the fact. Madelines are baked in special pans (available in many kitchenware stores) that are similar to shallow muffin pans, except the indentations are shaped like scallop shells. Thus, not only do they taste delectable but these little cakes are also most attractive. This chocolate version of Madelines is dark and rich, with a taste and texture similar to a brownie. One can only speculate as to the praise Proust would have accorded to these.

2 eggs
1 cup sugar
1 stick (½ cup) butter, melted
1 teaspoon vanilla
1 cup flour
⅓ cup unsweetened cocoa powder,
   sifted if necessary
⅛ teaspoon salt

Yield: 16 Madelines

1. Preheat the oven to 350°F.
2. Lightly grease a Madeline pan. (If you do not have a Madeline pan, you may bake the cakes in mini muffin tins, but the appearance will, of course, be different.)
3. In a large bowl, beat the eggs. Gradually beat in the sugar, continuing to beat until the mixture is thick and pale. Beat in the butter, then the vanilla.
4. In another bowl, stir together the flour, cocoa, and salt. Add to the egg mixture, stirring just until the dry ingredients are incorporated.
5. Bake the Madelines for about 15 minutes, or until a toothpick inserted in the center of a Madeline comes out clean. Let the Madelines cool slightly. Then remove from the pan and place on a rack to cool.

Greek Wedding Cookies

KOURAMABEDES

*T*hese rich cookies contain a substantial amount of butter and ground walnuts, and are wonderful in their traditional version. But, as I had suspected, the chocolate cookies are even better.

2 sticks (1 cup) butter or margarine, softened (try to use at least half butter if possible)

1½ cups confectioners' sugar

1 egg

1 tablespoon brandy

1 cup finely ground walnuts

2 cups flour

½ cup unsweetened cocoa powder, sifted if lumpy

additional confectioners' sugar for rolling the cookies

Yield: about 2 dozen cookies

1. In a large bowl, cream the butter with the sugar, continuing to beat until the sugar is fully incorporated. Beat in the egg, then the brandy and walnuts.
2. In another bowl, stir together the flour and cocoa. Add to the creamed mixture, beating or stirring until the dry ingredients are incorporated. Chill the dough for 1 hour, or until firm.
3. Preheat the oven to 350°F.
4. Grease two baking sheets.
5. Form the dough into balls, about 1½ inches in diameter, and place on the baking sheets. Bake the cookies for about 15 minutes, or until they are fully baked. (A toothpick inserted in the center of a cookie should come out clean.)
6. While still hot, roll the cookies in confectioners' sugar. Transfer to a rack to cool.

Dream Bars

*D*ream bars were very much the rage in the 1960s. Although most often encountered as Lemon Dream Bars, other fruit flavors were popular as well. The bars consist of a buttery cookie base, topped with a soft, rich filling, and then coated with a light glaze. These Dream Bars contain chocolate in the base, filling, and glaze, and are sufficiently delectable to warrant being in anyone's "dreams."

1 cup flour
1 stick (½ cup) butter or margarine, softened
½ cup confectioners' sugar
¼ cup unsweetened cocoa powder
1 cup granulated sugar
2 1-ounce squares unsweetened chocolate, melted
½ teaspoon baking powder
⅛ teaspoon salt
2 eggs
½ cup chocolate-flavored confectioners' sugar
4 teaspoons water

Yield: 16 servings

1. Preheat the oven to 350°F.
2. Grease and flour an 8-inch-square pan.
3. In a bowl, mix together the flour, butter, confectioners' sugar, and cocoa until the mixture is crumbly. Press into the prepared pan. Bake for 20 minutes.
4. Meanwhile, beat together the granulated sugar, melted chocolate, baking powder, salt, and eggs. When the cookie base has baked for 20 minutes, pour this mixture over it. Return to the oven and bake for 25 minutes longer, or until set. Transfer the baking pan to a rack to cool.
5. When the pan has cooled completely, stir together the chocolate-flavored confectioners' sugar and water until smooth, and spread over the filling. Cut into 16 squares.

Egg Yolk Cookies

*T*hese cookies constitute a clever way to use up egg yolks that are left over from another recipe, such as meringue or angel food cake. Chocolate Yolk Cookies are deliciously rich and buttery—guaranteed to vanish quickly!

1 **stick (½ cup) butter or magarine, softened (try to use at least half butter if possible)**
⅔ **cup sugar**
3 **egg yolks**
1 **teaspoon vanilla**
1⅓ **cups flour**
⅓ **cup unsweetened cocoa powder, sifted if lumpy**
about ½ **cup confectioners' sugar**

Yield: about 18 cookies

1. In a large bowl, cream the butter with the sugar, continuing to beat until the sugar is fully incorporated. Beat in the egg yolks, then the vanilla.
2. In another bowl, stir together the flour and cocoa. Add to the butter mixture, beating or stirring until the dry ingredients are incorporated. Chill the dough for 1 hour, or until firm.
3. Preheat the oven to 350°F.
4. Grease a large baking sheet.
5. Form the dough into balls, about 1 inch in diameter. Roll each ball in confectioners' sugar and shake to dislodge any excess sugar. Place the balls on the prepared baking sheet.
6. Bake the cookies for about 15 minutes. Transfer to a rack to cool.

Hermits

*N*o one seems to know how Hermits got their name, but all cookbooks agree that they are large spice cookies that contain plenty of raisins and walnuts. Chocolate hermits, always a favorite American cookie, are even more satisfying than any of the original versions.

10 tablespoons butter or margarine, softened
 1 cup brown sugar, preferably dark
 2 eggs
 ¼ cup water
 ¾ cup flour
 ¾ cup whole wheat flour
 ⅓ cup unsweetened cocoa powder, sifted if lumpy
 ½ teaspoon baking soda
 1 teaspoon cinnamon
 ¼ teaspoon ground cloves
 ¼ teaspoon nutmeg
 ⅛ teaspoon salt
 1 cup raisins
 1 cup chopped walnuts

Yield: 18 3-inch cookies

1. Preheat the oven to 375°F.
2. Grease two cookie sheets.
3. In a large bowl, cream the butter with the brown sugar, continuing to beat until the sugar is fully incorporated. Beat in the eggs, then the water.
4. In another bowl, stir together the flours, cocoa, baking soda, cinnamon, cloves, nutmeg, and salt. Add to the creamed mixture, beating or stirring until the dry ingredients are incorporated. Stir in the raisins and walnuts.
5. Drop the batter by heaping tablespoonfuls onto the prepared cookie sheets. (Each cookie should use a scant ¼ cup of dough.) Do not place too close together, as the cookies will spread while they bake.
6. Bake the cookies for 12 to 14 minutes, or until a toothpick inserted in a cookie comes out clean. Transfer the cookies to a rack to cool.

Jelly Tots

*J*elly Tots, also known as Thumbprint Cookies, were probably most popular in the 1950s. But this delicious, buttery cookie most definitely deserves a revival. And naturally, Chocolate Jelly Tots are even better than the original. Use any flavor of jelly, jam, or preserves that goes well with the taste of chocolate. I like raspberry, cherry, and apricot jams, as well as orange marmalade.

1 stick (½ cup) butter or margarine, softened
⅓ cup sugar
⅓ cup brown sugar, preferably dark brown
2 eggs, one of them separated
½ teaspoon vanilla
1 cup flour
⅓ cup unsweetened cocoa powder, sifted if lumpy
⅛ teaspoon salt
about ¼ cup jelly, jam, or marmalade (assorted if you wish)

Yield: 12 to 15 cookies

1. In a large bowl, cream the butter with the sugars, continuing to beat until the sugars are thoroughly incorporated. Beat in the egg, egg yolk, and vanilla.
2. In another bowl, stir together the flour, cocoa, and salt. Add to the creamed mixture, beating or stirring until the dry ingredients are incorporated. Chill the dough for about 1 hour, or until firm.
3. Preheat the oven to 350°F.
4. Grease two cookie or baking sheets.
5. Lightly beat the reserved egg white.
6. Form the dough into balls about 1½ inches in diameter, dip into the egg white, and place on the prepared baking sheets.
7. Bake the cookies for 8 minutes. Remove the cookies from the oven and make a depression in the center of each. Although you can use your thumb for this (hence the name "thumbprint cookies"), the dough is likely to be quite hot. A better method is to make the indentation with the handle of a wooden spoon. Fill the indentations with jelly.
8. Return the cookies to the oven and bake for 12 to 14 minutes longer, or until the cookies are done. Transfer to a rack to cool.

Oatmeal Cookies

*T*hese are the classic oatmeal cookies, a favorite of everyone's childhood, but with a dark chocolate dough and chocolate chips instead of the customary raisins.

1 stick (½ cup) butter or margarine, softened
¾ cup sugar
½ cup brown sugar, preferably dark brown
2 eggs
1 teaspoon vanilla
2 tablespoons milk
1 cup flour
⅓ cup unsweetened cocoa powder, sifted if lumpy
1 teaspoon baking powder
⅛ teaspoon salt
1 cup rolled oats
¾ cup semi-sweet chocolate morsels

Yield: about 30 2-inch cookies

1. Preheat the oven to 350°F.
2. Grease two large cookie sheets.
3. In a large bowl, cream the butter with the sugars, continuing to beat until they are fully incorporated. Beat in the eggs, then the vanilla and milk.
4. In another bowl, stir together the flour, cocoa, baking powder, and salt. Add to the creamed mixture, beating or stirring until the dry ingredients are incorporated. Stir in the oats and chocolate morsels.
5. Drop the dough into rounds about 1½ inches in diameter, allowing about 2 inches between the cookies for spreading while they bake.
6. Bake the cookies for 12 to 15 minutes, or until the bottoms are lightly browned and they are cooked through. They will be slightly soft when done baking but will firm up as they cool. Transfer the cookies to a rack.

No-Bake Chocolate Bars

Unbaked bars have been popular with children and adults since the advent of Rice Krispies-marshmallow bars. Adults like these bars because there's no baking involved and because their children can usually help in the preparation. The chocolate unbaked bars are more sophisticated than the cereal variety and contain three layers—a dark chocolate crumb crust, a caramel-like filling flavored with gingersnap crumbs, and a topping of melted chocolate. These are a guaranteed hit!

BOTTOM LAYER
  1 stick (½ cup) butter or margarine
  ½ cup sugar
  ¼ cup unsweetened cocoa powder
  2 cups chocolate cookie crumbs (use soft, home-style cookies, such as those made by Archway—wafer cookies are too dry for this recipe)

MIDDLE LAYER
  1 can sweetened condensed milk (not evaporated milk)
  2 tablespoons butter or margarine
  1 teaspoon vanilla
  ¾ cup coarsely crushed gingersnaps

TOPPING
  ¾ cup semi-sweet chocolate morsels, melted

Yield: 24 bars

1. Make the bottom layer: In a saucepan, cook the butter, sugar, and cocoa until the butter has melted and the mixture is smooth. Remove the pan from the heat and stir in the chocolate cookie crumbs. Firmly press the mixture onto the bottom of an 8- x 10-inch baking pan.

2. Make the middle layer: Place the sweetened condensed milk and butter in a saucepan. Bring to a boil, stirring. Then boil for 2 to 3 minutes, stirring well, so the mixture doesn't scorch. Remove the pan from the heat and stir in the vanilla and gingersnaps. Spread this mixture evenly over the chocolate crust. Let cool slightly.

3. Pour the melted chocolate over the caramel-like filling. Use a knife to spread it into a thin, even layer. Chill the pan until the bars are firm. Then cut into squares.

Wow!

IS THAT CHOCOLATE in my BREAD?

Bran Muffins

*T*his is probably the most nutritious dessert in this book; these muffins retain all the hearty, wholesome, good bran flavor. The only difference between these and ordinary muffins is that chocolate has been added to make them even darker and more flavorful. They make a wonderful between-meal snack!

¾ **cup flour**
½ **cup whole wheat flour**
½ **cup unsweetened cocoa powder, sifted if lumpy**
1 **teaspoon baking soda**
¼ **teaspoon salt**
2½ **cups bran cereal, such as Bran Buds**
2 **eggs, beaten**
¾ **cup sugar**
¼ **cup honey**
1½ **cups buttermilk, or place 1½ tablespoons vinegar in a measuring cup and add milk to come to the 1½-cup mark**
2½ **tablespoons vegetable oil**
½ **cup raisins**

Yield: 14 large muffins

1. Preheat the oven to 400°F.
2. Grease 14 muffin cups.
3. In a large bowl, stir together the flours, cocoa, baking soda, salt, and bran.
4. In another bowl, mix together the eggs, sugar, honey, buttermilk, and oil. Add to the bran mixture, stirring until the dry ingredients are moistened. Stir in the raisins.
5. Fill the muffin cups so the batter is level with the top of the cup. Bake the muffins for 20 to 25 minutes, or until a toothpick inserted in the center comes out clean. Remove the muffins from the tins and let cool on a rack.

Muffin Tops

*S*everal years ago, oversized muffins became the rage, and it was possible to find every variety imaginable. Then, some clever marketer, realizing that many people ate only the crispy tops of these large muffins and discarded the rest, started selling just the muffin tops. Now specialty muffin top pans are available in kitchenware shops, so anyone can easily whip up a batch. Muffin tops provide a cookie-like treat, letting you enjoy the best of the muffin without having to eat or waste the rest.

These chocolate-chocolate chip Muffin Tops are quite decadent. They make a great between-meal snack, accompanied by tea, coffee, or a glass of milk.

¾ **cup flour**

½ **cup whole wheat flour**

¾ **cup sugar**

⅓ **cup unsweetened cocoa powder, sifted if lumpy**

½ **teaspoon baking soda**

⅛ **teaspoon salt**

⅔ **cup buttermilk (or place 2 teaspoons vinegar in a measuring cup and add enough milk to come to the ⅔-cup mark)**

¼ **cup vegetable oil**

1 **egg, beaten**

½ **cup mini semi-sweet chocolate morsels**

Yield: 18 muffin tops

1. Preheat the oven to 350°F.
2. There is sufficient batter to make 18 muffin tops. Most muffin top pans make 12 muffin tops, so if you don't have two pans, you will need to bake the recipe in two batches. Grease your muffin top pan or pans.
3. In a large bowl, stir together the flours, sugar, cocoa, baking soda, and salt.
4. In another bowl, mix together the buttermilk, oil, and egg. Add to the dry ingredients and stir until the dry ingredients are moistened. Stir in the chocolate chips.
5. Divide the batter between the indentations in the muffin top pans, filling them so the batter is just level with the top of the pan. Bake the muffin tops for 15 to 18 minutes, or until a toothpick inserted in the center of a muffin top comes out clean.
6. Remove the muffin tops from the pan and transfer to a rack to cool.

Scones

Scones, originally from Scotland, are like extra-buttery biscuits; they are not too sweet, and make a wonderful accompaniment to tea. In recent years, scones have become very popular in this country. Although raisin scones are perhaps the most common, other varieties have proliferated. This recipe for Chocolate Scones produces pastries that are hearty and satisfying, particularly on a cold, wintry day.

1 cup flour
¾ cup whole wheat flour
2 teaspoons baking powder
¼ teaspoon salt
⅓ cup unsweetened cocoa powder, sifted if lumpy
⅓ cup plus 1 teaspoon sugar, divided
4 tablespoons butter
2 eggs
½ cup heavy or whipping cream

Yield: 8 scones

1. Preheat the oven to 450°F.
2. Grease a baking sheet.
3. In a large bowl, stir together the flours, baking powder, salt, cocoa, and ⅓ cup sugar. Using a pastry cutter, two knives, or your fingertips, work the butter into the dry ingredients, so the mixture is crumbly, and no lumps of butter remain.
4. In a small bowl, beat the eggs with the cream. Reserve 1 tablespoon of this mixture. Add the remainder of the egg mixture to the dry mixture and stir just until the dry ingredients are incorporated.
5. Place the dough on a lightly floured board and roll out to a round about ¾ inch thick (about 9 inches in diameter). Transfer to the prepared baking sheet. Cut the round into 8 equal-size wedges. Brush with the reserved egg mixture, and sprinkle with 1 teaspoon sugar.
6. Bake the scones for about 12 minutes, or until they are firm. Transfer to a rack to cool. Serve warm or at room temperature.

New Chocolate Classics

Swiss Egg Braids

EIER ZUPFEN

*T*his lovely yeasted bread is rich and chocolaty, with a slight hint of cinnamon. The texture is firm, rather like a pumpernickel bread, and it is not too sweet; it makes a wonderful way to enjoy the taste of chocolate other than for dessert. Like most yeast breads, this becomes stale after a day or two; use any leftovers to make a delicious bread pudding, following your favorite recipe.

DOUGH
- ⅓ cup scalded milk
- 1 cup sugar
- ⅓ cup unsweetened cocoa powder
- ½ teaspoon salt
- 1 package active dry yeast, dissolved in ¼ cup lukewarm water
- 2½ cups flour
- ½ stick (4 tablespoons) butter, melted
- 2 eggs

TOPPING
- 2 tablespoons sugar
- 1 tablespoon unsweetened cocoa powder
- ½ teaspoon cinnamon
- 1 egg yolk, beaten with 1 tablespoon water

Yield: 12 to 14 slices

1. In a large bowl, stir together the milk, sugar, cocoa, and salt. Stir in the yeast, then 1 cup flour.
2. Cover the bowl with plastic wrap and let sit in a warm spot for 45 minutes. Add the butter and eggs, and stir vigorously. Stir in another 1 cup flour. Cover again with plastic wrap and let sit for 10 minutes.
3. Beat in the final ½ cup flour. Cover the bowl and let the dough sit in the refrigerator several hours or overnight.
4. Grease a baking sheet.
5. Stir together the sugar, cocoa, and cinnamon and spread on a clean surface.
6. Divide the dough into thirds. Roll each third in the cinnamon mixture to a thick rope, about 13 inches long. Place the ropes side by side on the baking sheet and braid. Pinch the ends together to seal. Sprinkle with any remaining cinnamon mixture.
7. Cover the braid with plastic and let rise in a warm spot for 1 hour.
8. Preheat the oven to 350°F.
9. Brush the loaf generously with the egg yolk mixture. Bake for 25 to 30 minutes, or until a toothpick inserted in the center comes out clean. Transfer to a rack to cool.

Danish Coffee Cake

KRINGLE

Kringle is a Danish coffee cake that's lightly spiced with cardamom and filled with a mixture of raisins, almonds, and dark rum. It's not too sweet and makes a perfect accompaniment to morning or afternoon tea. Chocolate Kringle is even more appealing.

DOUGH
- 2 cups flour
- 1 envelope active dry yeast
- ½ teaspoon salt
- ⅛ teaspoon cardamom
- ½ cup sugar
- ½ cup milk
- 2 1-ounce squares unsweetened chocolate
- 2 tablespoons butter
- 1 egg

FILLING
- ¾ cup raisins
- ⅓ cup almonds
- ½ cup confectioners' sugar
- 2 tablespoons butter or margarine, softened
- 1 tablespoon dark rum

Yield: 10 servings

1. In a large bowl, stir together the flour, yeast, salt, cardamom, and sugar.
2. Place the milk, chocolate, and butter in a saucepan. Heat until the butter and chocolate have melted. Add to the bowl with the flour and stir vigorously until the dry ingredients are incorporated. Beat in the egg. Turn the dough out onto a lightly floured board, and knead until smooth and elastic.
3. Place the dough in a clean bowl, and cover with plastic wrap. Let the dough rise in a warm, draft-free spot for 1 hour.
4. Meanwhile, prepare the filling: Cover the raisins with water in a saucepan. Bring to a boil, and cook for 5 minutes. Drain the raisins well. Place the raisins and the almonds in a food processor and grind coarsely. Add the confectioners' sugar, butter, and rum, and process until smooth.
5. Grease a baking sheet.
6. Roll out the dough to a strip about 22 inches long by 5 inches wide. Spread with the filling, leaving a 1-inch border on all sides. Fold the dough lengthwise over the filling, and pinch to seal. Twist to form a pretzel shape. Transfer to the prepared pan.
7. Cover the dough with plastic wrap and let rise for 1 hour.

8. Shortly before the dough has finished rising, preheat the oven to 350°F.
9. Brush the dough with water. Bake for 25 to 30 minutes, or until lightly browned. Transfer the cake to a rack to cool.

Swedish Coffee Cake

VETEKRANS

*V*etekrans *is a Swedish coffee cake that's spiced with cardamom and filled with a honey-almond mixture. It makes a delicious choice for a Sunday brunch or afternoon tea. By adding chocolate, the* Vetekrans *becomes even more special. It's not overly sweet, yet is still dark and chocolaty.*

DOUGH
1¾ to 2 cups flour
¼ teaspoon salt
1 teaspoon ground cardamom
½ cup sugar
2 teaspoons active dry yeast
½ cup milk
2 1-ounce squares unsweetened chocolate
4 tablespoons butter or margarine
1 egg, beaten

FILLING
⅓ cup almonds
2½ tablespoons honey
1 tablespoon water

TOPPING
2 tablespoons sliced almonds

Yield: 8 servings

1. In a large bowl, stir together 1¾ cups flour, salt, cardamom, sugar, and yeast.
2. In a saucepan, heat the milk, chocolate, and butter until the milk is scalded and the butter and chocolate are melted. Add the contents of the saucepan to the flour mixture. Stir well. (The dough will be very stiff.) Cover the bowl, and let the dough rise in a warm, draft-free spot for 1 hour.
3. Add the egg to the dough, and knead the dough in the bowl, just to combine all ingredients well. The dough should be very sticky. If it is runny, knead in up to ¼ cup additional flour.
4. Place the bowl in the refrigerator and chill for 1½ hours.
5. Meanwhile, prepare the filling: In the food processor, pulverize the almonds with the honey and water. Set aside.
6. Grease a large baking sheet.
7. On a lightly floured surface, roll the dough to a rectangle about 14 inches long by 8 inches wide. Spread with the almond filling. Roll up the dough, jelly-roll style, beginning with a long edge. Place the dough on the prepared baking sheet, and form into a ring shape. Pinch the ends of the ring together. With a sharp knife, cut the dough at ½-inch intervals, almost to the center of the ring. Pick up

each segment and turn on its side. When all segments have been turned, the dough ring will be fanned out.

8. Cover the cake with plastic wrap and let rise for about 45 minutes.

9. Preheat the oven to 350°F.

10. Sprinkle the coffee cake with the almonds, and press them into the dough slightly. Bake the cake for about 30 minutes, or until it is browned. Transfer to a rack to cool.

Kugelhopf

Kugelhopf is a traditional yeasted raisin coffee cake from Germany. Rich and buttery, Kugelhopf is usually baked in a special pan (available in kitchenware shops) that is similar to a fluted Bundt pan but narrower and higher. Although the cake won't be quite as attractive, it will be just as delicious if baked in an ordinary Bundt tube pan.

This Kugelhopf has the satisfying richness of any chocolate dessert. Because it's a coffee cake, it's not too sweet, so it makes a wonderful treat for brunch or afternoon tea.

4 teaspoons dry sherry
⅔ cup golden raisins
1 stick (½ cup) butter, softened
½ cup sugar
2 eggs
½ cup unsweetened cocoa powder, sifted if lumpy
2 teaspoons active dry yeast
⅛ teaspoon salt
2½ cups flour
⅔ cup milk, heated to lukewarm
½ teaspoon vanilla

Yield: 16 servings

1. In a small bowl, stir together the sherry and raisins and let sit for about 1 hour.
2. In a large bowl, beat the butter with the sugar until the sugar is fully incorporated. Beat in the eggs.
3. In another bowl, stir together the cocoa, yeast, salt, and about 1 cup flour. Add to the butter mixture, along with the lukewarm milk and vanilla. Mix well. Add the rest of the flour, stirring vigorously, until incorporated into the batter completely.
4. Cover the bowl with plastic wrap and let the dough rise in a warm, draft-free spot for 1 hour.
5. Grease a Bundt or tube pan.
6. Punch down the dough and place it in the prepared pan. Cover with plastic wrap and let rise until double, about 1 hour.
7. Shortly before the dough finishes rising, preheat the oven to 350°F.
8. Bake the Kugelhopf for 10 minutes. Lower the oven temperature to 325°F and bake for about 35 minutes more, or until a toothpick inserted in the highest part of the cake comes out clean.
9. Transfer the pan to a rack to cool. When cool, remove the Kugelhopf from the pan. Let cool completely before slicing.

Focaccia

*A*s just about everyone knows, focaccia is similar to a pizza but with a thicker crust. (This is because the focaccia dough is allowed to rise before baking.) Focaccia has become so popular that I decided to develop a chocolate version, which is superb. It makes a wonderful offering at brunch or for tea.

1 **package active dry yeast**
¾ **cup warm water**
¼ **teaspoon salt**
2 **tablespoons vegetable oil**
⅓ **cup sugar**
⅓ **cup unsweetened cocoa powder**
2 **cups bread flour**
1 **16-ounce can pitted dark sweet cherries, drained well**
2 **tablespoons slivered almonds**

Yield: 10 to 12 servings

1. In a large bowl, dissolve the yeast in the water. Add the salt, oil, sugar, and cocoa. Stir well. Stir in the flour. Don't worry if the flour isn't entirely incorporated.
2. Turn the dough out onto a board and knead it until it is smooth and elastic and all the flour is incorporated.
3. Place the dough in a clean bowl. Cover with plastic wrap and let sit in a warm place until about double in size, about 1 hour.
4. Grease a 9- x 13-inch baking pan. Press the dough into a roughly shaped oval that nearly fills the pan. Sprinkle with the cherries and almonds. Cover with plastic wrap and let rise for another hour.
5. When the dough has nearly finished rising, preheat the oven to 350°F.
6. Press the cherries into the dough. Bake the focaccia for about 40 minutes. Transfer to a rack to cool. The focaccia may be served warm from the oven or later during the same day. While leftovers may be refrigerated, it will not be as good as on the day it was baked.

Schnecken

Schnecken is the German word for snails, *a pastry that, in this country, goes by various names including pecan roll-ups and cinnamon buns. But whatever you call them, Schnecken are even more delectable when the buttery rich dough is flavored with cocoa and the filling contains semi-sweet chocolate in addition to the usual pecans and cinnamon.*

Note: For easier handling, the dough must be chilled for several hours or overnight before filling and baking the Schnecken.

DOUGH
- **1 tablespoon active dry yeast**
- **¼ cup lukewarm water**
- **½ teaspoon sugar plus ⅓ cup, divided**
- **1 stick (½ cup) butter**
- **½ cup milk**
- **⅓ cup unsweetened cocoa powder**
- **2 eggs**
- **½ teaspoon salt**
- **3 cups flour**

FILLING
- **2 tablespoons butter, melted**
- **1 cup brown sugar, preferably dark, divided**
- **1 cup chopped pecans**
- **½ cup coarsely ground semi-sweet chocolate**
- **1 teaspoon cinnamon**

Yield: 12 Schnecken

1. Dissolve the yeast in the warm water. Add ½ teaspoon sugar, and let sit several minutes.
2. In the meanwhile, melt the butter in the milk. Do not let the temperature of the milk get above lukewarm.
3. Transfer the butter mixture to the bowl of an electric mixer. Beat in the cocoa, eggs, salt, and remaining ⅓ cup sugar. Then beat in the yeast. Beat in the flour, adding about a cup at a time. When done, the mixture will be stiff and sticky. Cover the bowl with plastic wrap and let sit in the refrigerator for several hours or overnight.
4. Brush the insides of 12 muffin cups with some of the melted butter. Sprinkle a teaspoon of the brown sugar in the bottom of each tin.
5. In a bowl, stir together the remaining brown sugar, pecans, chocolate, and cinnamon.
6. Roll the dough out on a floured board to a 12- x 16-inch rectangle. Spread the remaining melted butter over the dough, and sprinkle evenly with the chocolate-pecan mixture. Beginning with a long edge, roll up the dough, jelly-roll style. Cut into 12 equal slices and place each slice in a muffin cup.

7. Let the dough rise, uncovered, for 30 minutes in a warm, draft-free spot.
8. Meanwhile, preheat the oven to 350°F.
9. Bake the Schnecken for 15 minutes. Lower the heat to 325°F and bake for 15 to 20 minutes longer, or until a toothpick inserted in the dough comes out clean. Immediately turn the Schnecken out of the cups onto a sheet of waxed paper.

Panettone

*P*anettone is a yeasted Italian coffee cake, filled with nuts and dried fruits, that is traditionally served at Christmas. The bread is baked in a large can (such as a 28-ounce tomato can), and it rises well above the pan to form a large mushroom shape. Chocolate Panettone is richer than the plain version, yet is not overly sweet. It makes a wonderful offering at a holiday brunch.

about 2 cups bread flour
⅔ cup sugar
1 package active dry yeast
½ teaspoon salt
½ cup plus 2 teaspoons milk, divided
2 tablespoons butter
2 1-ounce squares unsweetened chocolate
2 eggs
1 teaspoon grated orange rind
¼ cup golden raisins
¼ cup chopped dried apricots
¼ cup dried cherries
2 tablespoons pine nuts
2 tablespoons chopped almonds
¼ cup chocolate-flavored confectioners' sugar

Yield: 1 loaf or about 12 slices Panettone

Note: If you own a bread machine, you can make the dough in it and then transfer the dough to the can to rise and bake.

1. In a large bowl, stir together 1 cup flour with the sugar, yeast, and salt.

2. In a saucepan, heat the ½ cup milk, butter, and chocolate until the butter and chocolate have melted and just a few very tiny bubbles are forming at the edge of the liquid.

3. Add the hot milk mixture to the bowl with the flour mixture and stir very well. Beat in the eggs and orange rind. Add additional flour, about one-quarter cup at a time, until the dough becomes very stiff. Turn the dough out onto a floured surface and knead, adding more flour as needed, until the dough is smooth and elastic.

4. Place the dough in a large, greased bowl, and let rise, covered, in a warm spot for about 1 hour, or until doubled in size.

5. Meanwhile, prepare the baking pan: Grease the inside of a clean 28-ounce can.

6. In a small bowl, stir together the raisins, apricots, cherries, pine nuts, and almonds. Add to the dough and knead to distribute the fruit. Form the dough into a large ball and place in the prepared pan. With a sharp knife, slash an X in the top of the dough. Cover the can with

plastic wrap and let the dough sit in a warm spot for about 25 minutes, or until it reaches the top of the can.

7. Preheat the oven to 350°F.

8. Bake the loaf for 50 minutes, or until a knife inserted in the center comes out clean. Transfer the can to a rack to cool. When completely cool, remove the bread from the can.

9. In a small bowl, stir together the confectioners' sugar and the remaining 2 teaspoons milk. Pour over the top of the Panettone and let the glaze drip down the sides.

Polish Coffee Cake

WEILKANOCNA BABKA

*T*his tube-shaped coffee cake has the texture and flavor of a giant chocolate muffin that's dotted with fruity yellow raisins. It is wonderful for breakfast or as a snack. Although the dough uses yeast as a rising agent, there's no kneading involved—the cake is as easy to make as one with baking powder, but just takes longer because of the rising.

1 stick (½ cup) butter or margarine, softened
1½ cups sugar
4 egg yolks
1 package yeast, dissolved in ¼ cup lukewarm water
1 teaspoon salt
½ teaspoon cinnamon
½ cup unsweetened cocoa powder, sifted if lumpy
1 cup lukewarm milk
3 cups flour
1 cup yellow raisins

Yield: 12 servings

1. In a large bowl, cream the butter with the sugar, continuing to beat until the sugar is fully incorporated. Beat in the egg yolks, then the yeast. Beat in the salt, cinnamon, cocoa, and milk. Beat in the flour, then add the raisins.
2. Cover the bowl with plastic wrap and let rise in a warm spot for 2 hours.
3. Grease a tube pan. Transfer the dough to the pan and let rise, covered, for 1 hour.
4. Preheat the oven to 350°F.
5. Bake the cake for about 1 hour, or until a toothpick inserted in the highest part of the cake comes out clean. Transfer the pan to a rack to cool.

Greek Sweet Bread

VASILOPITTA

*T*his braided bread is similar to Jewish challah, except that it contains spices. The chocolate version, being richer and sweeter, is delicious as a coffee cake or for brunch.

**1 package active dry yeast (about
   2½ teaspoons)**
2 tablespoons lukewarm water
⅔ cup lukewarm milk
3 cups flour, divided
1 teaspoon sugar plus ¾ cup, divided
2 eggs, beaten
½ stick (4 tablespoons) butter, melted
½ cup unsweetened cocoa powder
½ teaspoon salt
¼ teaspoon nutmeg
¼ teaspoon cinnamon
¼ teaspoon ground cloves
about 2 teaspoons sesame seeds

Yield: 12 to 16 slices

1. In a large bowl, stir together the yeast and water. Add the milk, ½ cup flour, and 1 teaspoon sugar. Cover the bowl and let sit in a warm place for 1 hour.
2. Add 2¼ cups flour, ¾ cup sugar, eggs, butter, cocoa, salt, nutmeg, cinnamon, and cloves to the bowl. Stir vigorously until mixed.
3. Turn the dough out onto a board and knead until smooth and no longer sticky, adding up to ¼ cup flour if needed.
4. Place the dough in a clean bowl. Cover and let rise in a warm spot for 1½ hours.
5. Grease a large baking sheet.
6. Divide the dough into thirds. Roll each third into a rope about 18 inches long. Place side by side on the baking sheet and braid. Pinch the ends together tightly. Cover the bread and let rise in a warm spot for 1 hour.
7. Preheat the oven to 375°F.
8. Brush the loaf with water and sprinkle with the sesame seeds.
9. Bake the bread for 25 to 30 minutes. Transfer to a rack to cool.

Zwieback

Zwieback is toasted bread that's most commonly used as a food for teething babies. Homemade Zwieback is as delicious as biscotti and, in fact, is made like biscotti, except with a bread dough rather than a cookie dough. Chocolate Zwieback is especially wonderful for dipping into a cup of hot coffee or tea.

If you own a bread maker, the dough can be made in the machine, which is easier than making it by hand.

2½ cups flour
½ cup unsweetened cocoa powder
½ teaspoon salt
⅔ cup sugar
2 teaspoons active dry yeast
¾ cup milk
2½ tablespoons butter or margarine
1 egg, beaten

Yield: 24 Zwieback

1. In a large bowl, stir together the flour, cocoa, salt, sugar, and yeast. In a small saucepan, heat the milk and butter, stirring until the butter melts. Add to the flour mixture. Add the egg. Mix with your hands and then knead until the mixture forms a smooth, elastic dough.
2. Place the dough in a clean bowl. Cover with plastic wrap and let rise in a warm draft-free spot for 1 hour.
3. Grease two 9- x 5-inch loaf pans. Divide the dough into two pieces and spread each piece on the bottom of each pan. (The dough will be only about 1 inch high.) Cover the pans and let rise for 45 minutes. (The loaves will be less than 2 inches high.)
4. When nearly done rising, preheat the oven to 350°F.
5. Bake the bread for 25 minutes and let cool completely.
6. Preheat the oven to 250°F.
7. Cut the loaves into ½-inch slices and lay the slices on their sides on a baking sheet. Bake until crisp and completely dry, about 1¾ hours.

Waffles

*E*veryone loves waffles, and chocolate waffles are positively the best, especially when topped with a scoop of vanilla ice cream and Warm Chocolate Syrup. Waffles are very easy to make—all you need is a waffle iron.

WARM CHOCOLATE SYRUP

¾ cup water
½ cup sugar
2 1-ounce squares unsweetened chocolate
1 teaspoon vanilla

WAFFLES

2 eggs
⅓ cup sugar
¼ cup vegetable oil
1 cup milk
1 cup flour
¼ cup unsweetened cocoa powder, sifted if lumpy
1½ teaspoons baking powder
¼ teaspoon salt

Yield: 2 large waffles (4 squares each); 2 very generous servings or 4 average servings

1. First, make the syrup. Place the water and sugar in a small heavy saucepan. Bring to a boil, stirring to dissolve the sugar. Boil gently for 5 to 7 minutes, without stirring. Remove the pan from the heat and add the chocolate. Stir until melted. If the syrup is too thin, cook a little longer until of desired consistency. Stir in the vanilla. Keep warm while preparing the waffles.

2. Preheat a waffle iron according to the manufacturer's directions.

3. In a large bowl, beat the eggs. Gradually beat in the sugar, continuing to beat until the mixture is thick and pale. Beat in the oil, then the milk.

4. In another bowl, stir together the flour, cocoa, baking powder, and salt. Add to the egg mixture, stirring only until the large lumps are mixed in. The batter should not be overmixed.

5. Cook the waffles according to the instructions provided by the manufacturer. Serve immediately, topped with Warm Chocolate Syrup and ice cream, if desired.

UNIQUELY CHOCOLATE CREATIONS

Divinity

*O*ne taste of this luscious candy and you'll know why its name is derived from the word "divine." Divinity is like a low-fat, whipped fudge and tastes similar to a finer version of the Tootsie Roll. With a candy thermometer, Divinity is very easy to prepare.

½ **cup water**
½ **cup light corn syrup**
2 **cups sugar**
3 **1-ounce squares unsweetened chocolate**
2 **egg whites, at room temperature**

Yield: about 1¾ pounds of candy or about 24 1½-inch balls

1. Place the water, corn syrup, sugar, and chocolate in a heavy saucepan with a handle. Bring the ingredients to a boil, stirring until the chocolate has melted. After the mixture reaches a boil, place the lid on the saucepan and cook for 3 minutes. (This will dissolve any sugar crystals that have adhered to the side of the saucepan.)

2. Uncover the saucepan and cook, without stirring, until the mixture reaches 254°F (hard-ball stage).

3. While the mixture is cooking, beat the egg whites until somewhat stiff.

4. After the mixture has reached 254°F, add it to the egg whites very gradually, beating the whole time with an electric mixer on low speed. Do not scrape the saucepan.

5. With the electric mixer on high speed, beat the candy until it can be dropped onto waxed paper in a ball that holds its shape. The mixture will start out very shiny and dark brown. When it has been beaten sufficiently, the candy will turn a lighter shade of brown and become less shiny.

6. Immediately drop the candy by spoonfuls onto waxed paper, forming each into a ball-like shape, about 1½ inches in diameter. About 5 minutes after dropping the candy (when cool enough to handle), roll each piece in your hands to form a smooth ball. When fully cooled, store the candy in an airtight container at room temperature.

New Chocolate Classics

Marshmallows

*H*omemade marshmallows have a far better flavor and texture than the store-bought variety. Chocolate marshmallows are especially delicious and well loved by children.

Note: I haven't yet tested how well homemade marshmallows fare when cooked on a stick over an open flame.

3 envelopes unflavored gelatin
⅔ cup water, divided
2 cups sugar
½ cup light corn syrup
¼ teaspoon salt
3 1-ounce squares unsweetened chocolate
1 teaspoon vanilla
unsweetened cocoa powder (about ⅓ cup)

Yield: about 1¼ pounds candy

1. In a large bowl, stir together the gelatin and ⅓ cup water. Let sit for 30 minutes.
2. Place the remaining ⅓ cup water, sugar, corn syrup, salt, and chocolate in a large heavy saucepan. Bring to a boil, stirring often. Cover the pot and simmer for 3 minutes. Remove the pot cover and let the mixture boil, undisturbed, until it reaches 240 to 244°F (soft-ball stage).
3. Gradually pour the hot syrup over the gelatin mixture, beating constantly with an electric mixer. Continue beating for another 7 to 8 minutes, or until the mixture is thick. Beat in the vanilla.
4. Sprinkle the bottom of an 8-inch-square pan with the cocoa, and pour in the candy mixture. It will be very sticky. Let the pan sit at room temperature, uncovered, for 12 to 18 hours.
5. With a knife, loosen the marshmallow mixture from the sides of the pan. Dust your hands with the cocoa. Then, using your hands, pull the mixture out of the pan (it will stay in one piece) and transfer it to a cutting board dusted with cocoa. With a sharp knife dipped in cocoa, cut the candy into 1-inch squares. Roll each square in cocoa. Store the marshmallows in a covered tin.

Toffee

*A*lmost everyone knows toffee as the immensely popular Heath Bars. Homemade toffee, though, is even more delicious, especially when it's chocolate flavored!

Making candy is easy if you have a cooking thermometer—and quite a bit trickier if you don't. Since these thermometers are very inexpensive, it's best to buy one, and then you can make candy anytime you wish.

**8 ounces (about 2 cups) slivered
   blanched almonds**
2¼ cups sugar
  ⅓ cup light corn syrup
  **4 1-ounce squares unsweetened
    chocolate**
  ¼ cup water
  2 sticks (1 cup) butter
  4 ounces milk chocolate

Yield: about 2 pounds candy

1. Place the almonds in a heavy skillet. Cook over a medium heat, stirring frequently, until the nuts are golden brown. Remove from the skillet immediately or they will burn as they continue to toast.
2. Lightly grease an 11- by 16-inch jelly-roll pan.
3. In a large, heavy saucepan, place the sugar, corn syrup, unsweetened chocolate, and water. Cook over a medium heat, stirring occasionally, until the mixture comes to a boil. Add the butter. Continue cooking, stirring frequently, until the mixture reaches 300°F on a candy thermometer. (This is the "hard-crack" stage.) Remove the pan from the heat and stir in all but ⅓ cup almonds. Immediately pour the candy mixture into the prepared pan, spreading it into an even layer. (Be very careful because it is exceedingly hot.) The mixture will begin to harden quickly, so you will need to work fast.
4. Transfer the pan to a rack and let it cool completely.
5. Melt the milk chocolate. Using a knife, spread the chocolate in an even layer over the toffee. Sprinkle with the remaining almonds. Place the pan in the refrigerator until the milk chocolate has hardened.
6. Using the point of a knife, break the toffee into pieces. Store in a tin with waxed paper between the layers.

Semi-Freddo

*T*his is a type of Italian ice cream that requires no special equipment. Usually vanilla flavored, semi-freddo gets its richness from heavy cream and lightness from stiffly beaten egg whites. Chocolate Semi-Freddo is truly magnificent.

6 egg whites

2 cups heavy or whipping cream

1⅔ cups confectioners' sugar

⅔ cup unsweetened cocoa powder, sifted if lumpy

½ cup coarsely grated semi-sweet chocolate

1 recipe Fudge Sauce from Fettuccine with Fudge Sauce (page 150)

Yield: 10 to 12 servings

1. Line a 9- x 5-inch loaf pan with aluminum foil. Set aside.
2. In a large bowl, beat the egg whites until stiff. Set aside.
3. In another large bowl, beat the heavy cream until thick. Beat in the confectioners' sugar, then the cocoa. Fold in the chocolate, then the beaten egg whites.
4. Pour the mixture into the prepared pan. Cover with foil and freeze for several hours or until firm.
5. To serve the semi-freddo, turn the mixture out of the pan and remove the foil. Cut the loaf into slices about ½ inch thick. Place each slice on a serving plate and cover with a generous spoonful of Fudge Sauce.

Baked Alaska

Baked Alaska is a very 1950s dessert that has fallen out of style. For those unfamiliar with Baked Alaska, the dessert is comprised of a cake layer, which is covered by a mound of ice cream. This is frozen solid and, just before serving, coated with a layer of meringue. The entire dessert is placed in a very hot oven long enough to brown the meringue without melting the ice cream. The combination of warm cake, cold ice cream, and melting meringue—all topped with hot fudge sauce—is truly irresistible.

If regular Baked Alaska makes a spectacular dessert, Chocolate Baked Alaska is even more appealing. A thin layer of ground almonds and raspberry jam between the chocolate cake and ice cream lends a subtle counterpoint taste.

CAKE LAYER

- 1 stick (½ cup) butter or margarine, softened
- 1 cup sugar
- 1 egg
- ½ teaspoon vanilla
- ½ cup buttermilk (or place 1½ teaspoons vinegar in a measuring cup and add milk to the ½-cup mark)
- 1 cup flour
- ¼ cup unsweetened cocoa powder, sifted if lumpy
- ½ teaspoon baking soda
  pinch of salt

FILLING

- ½ cup ground almonds
- 3 tablespoons seedless raspberry jam
- 1 tablespoon dark rum
- 2 pints premium chocolate ice cream, slightly softened

MERINGUE

- 4 egg whites
- ⅔ cup sugar
- 1 tablespoon unsweetened cocoa powder

1. Preheat the oven to 375°F.
2. Grease and flour a 9-inch-round layer cake pan.
3. In a large bowl, cream the butter with the sugar, continuing to beat until the sugar is fully incorporated. Beat in the egg, then the vanilla and buttermilk.
4. In another bowl, stir together the flour, cocoa, baking soda, and salt. Add to the creamed mixture, beating or stirring until the dry ingredients are incorporated.
5. Spread the mixture evenly in the prepared pan. Bake the cake for 25 to 30 minutes, or until a toothpick inserted in the center comes out clean. Transfer the pan to a rack to cool. When cool, remove the cake from the pan and place, top side up, on a baking pan or ovenproof platter.
6. Stir together the ground almonds, raspberry jam, and rum. Spread the mixure over the top of the cake. Using a large spoon, mound the ice cream over the cake, to form a domelike shape. Cover the ice cream with foil or plastic wrap and freeze for several hours, or until completely frozen.
7. Prepare the Fudge Sauce.
8. Shortly before serving the Baked Alaska, preheat the oven to 475°F.

To Serve
1 recipe Fudge Sauce from Fettuccine
with Fudge Sauce (page 150)

Yield: 8 servings

9. In a large bowl, beat the egg whites until stiff. Gradually beat in the sugar, continuing to beat until the mixture is thick and glossy. Beat in the cocoa.

10. Spread the meringue evenly over the ice cream, covering both the ice cream and the cake completely. Place the Baked Alaska in the oven for 3 to 4 minutes, just until the meringue browns lightly.

11. Serve the Baked Alaska immediately, accompanied by hot Fudge Sauce.

Uniquely Chocolate Creations

Zabaglione

Zabaglione, made with lots of egg yolks, must be one of the richest desserts imaginable. Although many Italian restaurants serve Zabaglione on its own in tall, parfait-like glasses, I think the dessert is better as a rich sauce, spooned over fresh fruit or pound cake. Chocolate Zabaglione, which is like an incredibly rich fudge sauce, also makes a wonderful topping for brownies.

Zabaglione is traditionally served immediately after it has been made, in order to experience its unique combination of richness, warmth, and airy texture. The chocolate version is so good, though, no one would complain about receiving a cold portion of Zabaglione that had been refrigerated and served a day or two later.

4 egg yolks
1 cup confectioners' sugar
¼ cup unsweetened cocoa powder
½ cup Marsala wine

Yield: 4 servings

1. Place the egg yolks, confectioners' sugar, and cocoa in the top of a double boiler over boiling water. Using a wire whisk, beat the mixture until it is frothy. Gradually, add the Marsala, continuing to beat all the while.
2. Continue cooking the Zabaglione, while beating it, until the mixture has doubled in volume and has thickened somewhat. Remove from the heat and serve immediately.

New Chocolate Classics

Italian Cheesecake

Italian cheesecake—made with ricotta rather than cream cheese—is less rich than its American counterpart, yet is completely satisfying. This luxurious chocolate cheesecake contains pine nuts, golden raisins, and aromatic spices.

2 pounds whole milk ricotta cheese

6 eggs

1½ cups sugar

2 teaspoons vanilla

6 1-ounce squares unsweetened chocolate, melted

⅓ cup flour

½ teaspoon cinnamon

¼ teaspoon nutmeg

⅛ teaspoon salt

½ cup pine nuts

½ cup golden raisins

Yield: 20 servings

1. Preheat the oven to 300°F.
2. Grease a 9- x 13-inch baking pan.
3. In a large bowl, beat the ricotta cheese until smooth. Beat in the eggs, then the sugar and vanilla. Beat in the chocolate.
4. In a small bowl, stir together the flour, cinnamon, nutmeg, and salt. Beat into the ricotta mixture. Stir in the pine nuts and raisins.
5. Spread the cheese mixture evenly in the prepared pan. Bake the cheesecake for 1¼ hours, or until a toothpick inserted in the center comes out clean. Transfer the cheesecake to a rack to cool. This cake is best served at room temperature on the day it is made. Leftovers should be refrigerated.

Fettuccine with Fudge Sauce

*B*efore you think this dessert is too bizarre to even consider trying, I want to tell you about the Fancy Food Show. This event, held for culinary professionals, takes place annually and features several hundred companies, each providing samples of their food offerings. The main purpose of the Fancy Food Show is to introduce new products to restaurateurs and owners of gourmet food stores.

Given that the show has a few hundred booths and several thousand foods to sample, there is virtually no waiting to taste the foods at any given booth. In fact, it is almost impossible to visit every booth, much less to taste all the wonderful foods that each company features.

So I was surprised to see a long line snaking away from a single booth at the show. When I investigated, I saw that everyone was standing in line (for as long as half an hour) to taste chocolate fettuccine with fudge sauce.

So I decided to develop a chocolate pasta and fudge sauce recipe. If you do not wish to make your own fresh pasta, I have occasionally spotted dry chocolate pasta in specialty food stores. (It is also available by mail from Schenone Specialty Foods in California. Call 800-760-CHOC.) The Fudge Sauce is a wonderful, all-purpose chocolate fudge sauce that is great over ice cream and is easy to prepare and can be reheated over and over again.

FETTUCCINE
- 1⅓ **cups flour**
- ⅓ **cup unsweetened cocoa powder**
- ⅓ **cup sugar**
- ¼ **teaspoon salt**
- 1 **egg, mixed with enough water to equal a total of ⅓ cup plus 2 tablespoons (or use 12 to 16 ounces packaged chocolate pasta)**

Yield: 6 to 8 servings

1. Place the flour, cocoa, sugar, and salt in the pasta maker, and process until mixed. With the pasta maker running, gradually add the egg-water mixture. Follow the manufacturer's instructions as to when the pasta is ready to be extruded, making the pasta in a fettuccine shape. Refrigerate or freeze if not cooking that day.
2. Shortly before eating, bring a large pot of water to a boil. Add the fettuccine, and boil until cooked al dente. The fresh homemade pasta will take only 2 to 3 minutes to cook, while the dried pasta will take 5 minutes, or longer.
3. While the pasta is cooking, prepare the Fudge Sauce.
4. Drain the pasta well, and serve with Fudge Sauce.

FUDGE SAUCE

**4 1-ounce squares unsweetened
 chocolate**
1 cup sugar
⅛ teaspoon salt
1 tablespoon butter
1 cup light cream or half and half
½ teaspoon vanilla

Yield: about 2 cups sauce

1. In a medium-size saucepan, melt the chocolate over very low heat. Stir in the sugar, salt, butter, and cream. Cook over very low heat, stirring, about 5 minutes. Do not let the mixture boil.
2. Remove from the heat and stir in the vanilla. Serve warm over the fettuccine.

Queso Fresco Crepes

*T*his Mexican dessert, which translates to Fresh Cheese Crepes, uses ricotta cheese as a filling for light French crepes. Here the crepes are chocolate flavored, and the ricotta is blended with semi-sweet chocolate, which melts lusciously when the dessert is baked. The apricot sauce provides a fruity complement to the richness of the cheese filling.

CREPES
- ¾ cup plus 2 tablespoons flour
- 6 tablespoons sugar
- 3 tablespoons unsweetened cocoa powder
- pinch of salt
- 2 eggs
- 1 cup milk
- ⅓ cup water
- 2 tablespoons butter, melted

FILLING
- 1 15-ounce container ricotta cheese
- ¼ cup sugar
- 1 cup coarsely ground semi-sweet chocolate

SAUCE
- ½ cup apricot jam
- 1 tablespoon butter

Yield: 12 crepes or 6 servings

1. First make the crepes: In a bowl, stir together the flour, sugar, cocoa, and salt. Add the eggs and mix well. Using a wire whisk, beat in the milk, then the water, then the melted butter. Cover the bowl, and place in the refrigerator for 1 to 2 hours.

2. Heat a crepe pan or other 7-inch skillet. Spray with no-stick cooking spray. Pour ¼ cup batter into the skillet and swirl to cover the bottom evenly. Cook approximately 45 seconds. Then turn the crepe and cook about 45 seconds on the other side. Turn out of the skillet onto a sheet of waxed paper. Continue cooking the crepes until all the batter has been used.

3. Preheat the oven to 325°F.

4. Grease a 9- x 13-inch baking pan.

5. Mix together the ricotta cheese, sugar, and ground chocolate. Divide evenly among the crepes, filling the center third of each crepe. Roll up each crepe, and place, seam side down, in a single layer in the pan.

6. Bake the crepes, uncovered, for 10 minutes.

7. Meanwhile, heat together the apricot jam and butter, stirring until the butter has melted. When the crepes have baked, drizzle the sauce over them. Serve immediately.

INDEX